BOOK · 4

SADDLERY

COLLEGE

THE MANUAL OF
STABLE MANAGEMENT

COMPILED BY
Pat Smallwood FBHS

THE ADVISORY PANEL INCLUDED
Stewart Hastie MRCVS
Jeremy Houghton-Brown B Phil Ed
Sydney Free
Tessa Martin-Bird FBHS
Barbara Slane-Fleming FBHS
Helen Webber FBHS

SERIES EDITOR
Jane Kidd

First published 1989
Reprinted in enlarged format 1991, 1993
© British Horse Society 1989

British Library Cataloguing in Publication Data

British Horse Society manual of stable
management.
Bk. 4. Saddlery
1. Livestock : Horses. Management
I. British Horse Society, *Advisory Panel*
636.1'083

ISBN 1 872082 08 4

Produced for The British Horse Society by
The Kenilworth Press Ltd, Addington, Buckingham, MK18 2JR

Typeset by Rapid Communications Ltd, London WC1
Printed and bound in Great Britain

CONTENTS

Introduction

The aim of this series is to provide a reliable source of information and advice on all practical aspects of horse and stable management. Throughout the series emphasis is placed on the adoption of correct and safe procedures for the welfare of all who come into contact with horses, as well for the animals themselves.

The books have been compiled by a panel of experts, each drawing on considerable experience and contributing specialised knowledge on his or her chosen subject.

The other titles in the series are:

Book 1, The Horse – Conformation; Action; Psychology of the Horse; Teeth and Ageing; Breeds; Breeding; Identification; Buying and Selling; Glossary of Terms.

Book 2, Care of the Horse – Handling the Horse; Stable Vices and Problem Behaviour; Grooming; Bedding; Clipping, Trimming, Pulling and Plaiting; Recognising Good Health and Caring for the Sick Horse; Internal Parasites; Shoeing.

Book 3, The Horse at Grass – Grassland Management; Management of Horses and Ponies at Grass; Working the Grass-kept Pony or Horse; Bringing a Horse up from Grass.

Book 5, Specialist Care of the Competition Horse Dressage Horse; Driving Horse; Show Jumper; Event Horse; Long-Distance Horse; Hunter; Show Horse or Pony; Point-to-Pointer; Polo Pony; Types of Transportation; Travelling.

Book 6, The Stable Yard – Construction; Riding Schools; Organising and Running a Yard; The Buying of Fodder and Bedding; The Law.

Book 7, Watering and Feeding – Watering; Natural Feeding; The Digestive System; Principles of Feeding; Foodstuffs; Rations; Problem Eaters; The Feedshed, Storage and Bulk Purchasing.

NOTE: Throughout the book the term 'horses' is used and it will often include ponies.

CHAPTER 1
The Saddle

LEATHER

Most leather used for saddlery comes from the skin or hide of cows. To meet the demands of the saddlery and leather trade, much of it is imported. *Pigskin*, which is tough, elastic, and of light substance or thickness, is used in the making of the saddle seat. *Doeskin* is also occasionally used for saddle seats.

Tanning

The hide requires considerable preparation before it is ready for use. The process is known as tanning and currying. It takes many weeks, as much of it is done by hand and cannot be hurried: which is one of the reasons why good-quality leather can never be cheap.

The skin is first cleaned of hair, and then the texture is improved, strengthened and made more waterproof by the tanning process, which involves the use of lime, chemicals and greases. The skin, can now be described as leather, and is ready for dressing by the currier. Oils and greases are incorporated into it to improve its tensile strength, flexibility, and water-resistant properties. The hide should have plenty of substance – i.e. thickness – thus ensuring that it will last and will also stay flexible, because of the greater fat content of the leather.

Oak bark tanning is a vegetable process using tannin or

tanic acid produced from tree bark. It is considered one of the best methods of producing first-class leather.

Texture
Leather has a grain or outer side, and a flesh or inner side. The *grain side* is shiny, and is sealed to make it more water-proof; it is therefore less absorbent to any soap or dressing. The *flesh side* is unsealed, and has a rough, dull surface. It is less smooth, and is the side of the leather (except for the underneath lining of the saddle) which is usually next to the horse's skin. In use it loses fat and oil, and this is the side which, being more absorbent, should receive greater care during cleaning.

Colour
The colour of leather can be varied during the tanning process, but is confirmed by the use of dyes during curing. The most widely used colours are LONDON TAN which is yellow, HAVANA which is the colour of a good cigar, and WARWICK which is much darker.

Types of Leather
RAWHIDE is cowhide which has undergone a special vegetable tanning process. This makes the leather very strong and leaves a light, untanned central strip. Rawhide is used for stirrup leathers, girth straps, etc.
BUFFALO HIDE stirrup leathers are red in colour, greasy and soft to the touch. They are exceptionally strong and last many years, but they usually stretch.
CHROME-TANNED LEATHER is pale, blue-grey, and is produced by using salts of chromium. It is very strong, withstands wet, and remains supple. It is often used for New Zealand rug straps.
HELVETIA LEATHER is yellow in colour, and very greasy and tough. It is often used for reinforcing martingales, nosebands, etc.
BLACK LEATHER is also produced for the saddlery trade. It is generally used for harness, but is also fashionable with dressage riders.

Quality

When buying saddlery, it is important to be able to judge the quality of leather. Good leather should have plenty of substance, unless a special request has been made for a lighter weight – e.g. show bridles and racing saddles. This light type of leather wears much more quickly than a heavier sample.

Good leather should feel slightly greasy but firm. When bent in the hand, neither side should form bubbles on the skin. The grain or sealed side should not crack.

When examining a bridle, note that the flesh or unsealed side of the leather should be smooth in texture, with no rough fibres visible. Poor leather, seen in a cheap bridle, has rough edges and may feel spongy. Such bridles often have poor-quality fittings.

STRUCTURE OF THE SADDLE

The Saddle Tree

The tree is the framework around which the saddle is built. Trees were traditionally made from beech wood, but this has now been superseded by laminated wood, which is bonded under pressure, and then moulded to the required shape. The resulting tree is both lighter and stronger. Other materials, such as fibreglass and plastic, are also used, though these are not as easy to work with as laminated wood. Fibreglass is exceptionally strong and light, and is used in some racing saddles. Plastic appears to lack strength, and another disadvantage is that nails or tacks cannot be driven into it.

Trees are made in different shapes and sizes according to the intended use, the shape of the horse, and the preference of the rider. The shape of the tree dictates the main outline of the saddle.

Trees can be either rigid or 'sprung'. The RIGID TREE has a larger, more solid framework than the spring tree.

The Saddle

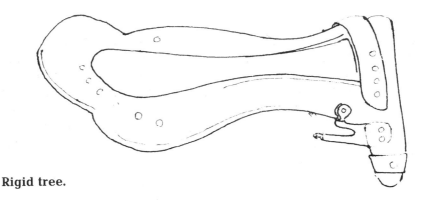

Rigid tree.

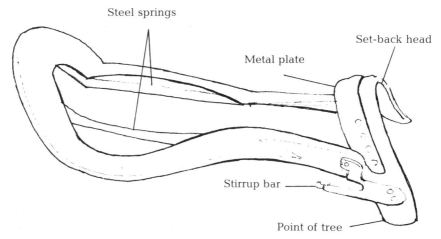

Steel springs

Set-back head

Metal plate

Stirrup bar

Point of tree

Spring tree.

The SPRING TREE has two flat panels of steel, which run from the underneath of the pommel to the cantle, and are set to lie about 5cms (2ins) on the inside of the broadest part of the seat. These steel panels are thin enough to give greater resilience to the seat of the saddle, and a more direct communication between the seat of the rider and the horse's back. On occasions, there can be a risk of damage to the back, and it is advisable always to use a numnah. The pommels of both types of saddle are reinforced on top and underneath with steel plates. For very heavy work, they can be reinforced.

10

The Stirrup Bars

The bars, which should be of hand-forged steel, are riveted to the points of the tree ● 'Cast' stirrup bars are found on cheap saddles, and their strength is suspect. The words 'forged' or 'cast' can be found stamped on the bar ● The bar itself should be of the regulation type and straight ● There has been discussion as to whether the safety-catch hinged on the bar is of any value. It is suggested that the length of the bar should be slightly extended, and with a slight upward curve. As yet, the Saddlers' Association has not come to a decision ● Hinged and turned-over stirrup bars were used once, but are now rarely seen. They were generally more troublesome than useful ● Recessed bars are used on most spring tree saddles, and on some rigid trees. They are placed under, rather than on top of, the tree, so there is less bulk to the stirrup leather under the rider's leg ● The bars on jumping saddles are placed well forward, and on dressage saddles they are positioned further back.

The Seat

Pre-strained webbing is fixed from the pommel to the cantle, and over this is placed stretched canvas or linen. Bellies – short pieces of felt or leather – are placed round the broadest part of the seat to support the edge. Serge is stretched down to form the seat shape. Wool, plastic foam or foam rubber are added to give resilience and extra cover to the tree, so that the rider cannot feel it through the seat. Of these three materials wool is most popular, and lasts indefinitely. In time, foam rubber disintegrates.

Pigskin or hide is then stretched on as the final seat cover with attached skirts. The SADDLE FLAPS are attached, followed by the GIRTH STRAPS. Two of the girth straps should be fixed to the web strap. The third strap is fixed independently. Girth straps should be of best-quality leather, as its strength and attachment are vital to the safety of the rider.

The Underneath Panels

These panels vary in design. The *full panel* gives a greater weight-bearing surface, and is probably the most comfortable for the horse as it makes the waist wider: but this can be uncomfortable for the rider. The *side panel* must be kept thin to allow the rider a close contact with the horse's sides. *Continental-type panels* are narrow at the waist and allow the rider a much closer contact. They go by various names and are used on all modern deep-seated saddles, together with knee and thigh rolls. The *short, or half, panel* is now mainly used in the cheaper pony and cob saddles. It has no knee or thigh rolls and does not help the rider as much as the other types to establish a balanced position. As there is less bulk under the leg, allowing a closer contact than a full panel, it is also used for show and polo saddles. .

Girth Straps

Many modern saddles, in particular those for dressage, have long girth straps to avoid bulk under the knee and thigh. These saddles require a shorter girth. The design is not as suitable for cross-country riding and hunting, as the straps are difficult to adjust from the saddle and are more likely to cause sores from mud around the buckle and guard area. They must be adjusted so that the buckles are clear of the elbow.

Linings

SERGE absorbs sweat but does not wear well and is the most difficult material to keep clean.

LINEN is easy to clean and wears longer than serge but not as long as leather.

LEATHER is easy to clean and wears well, as long as it is well looked after. Most good modern saddles are now lined with leather.

For saddles used without a numnah, linen and serge are both more absorbent of sweat and are therefore more comfortable for the horse and if well looked after are less likely to cause saddle problems.

Note that, when first put on, a leather lining can be cold to the back of a sensitive horse.

TYPES OF SADDLE

The main types of saddle are:

Jumping
This saddle is shaped to help the rider stay in balance when riding in a forward position over a jump. It has forward-cut flaps to accommodate the knees of the rider with his relatively short leg position, and it has appropriately placed knee and thigh rolls to assist in maintaining the leg position. The depth of seat varies: the choice depending on the individual's style of riding – some riders favouring a much deeper seat position.

Dressage
This saddle helps the rider to sit with a deep seat and a long leg. The saddle flap is cut much straighter, with only a slight curve in front. The stirrup bar is placed further back than on a jumping saddle. The saddle flap may need to be correspondingly longer, so that it does not catch the top of a tall rider's boot. The seat is deep, and the knee and thigh rolls are placed so as to assist the leg position.

General Purpose
This saddle is a combination of the above two types, with a less forward-cut flap. It is the saddle used by the majority of riders who do not wish to specialise.

Showing
This saddle has only a very slight forward-cut flap and the seat is relatively flat. It is always used without a numnah, so the fitting is of even more than usual importance.

Long Distance
Special saddles are now available which are designed to spread the rider's weight over as wide an area as possible so that pressure points are minimised. Their design incorporates features of the cavalry and western saddles, and they are placed over very thick, specially designed numnahs.

13

The Saddle

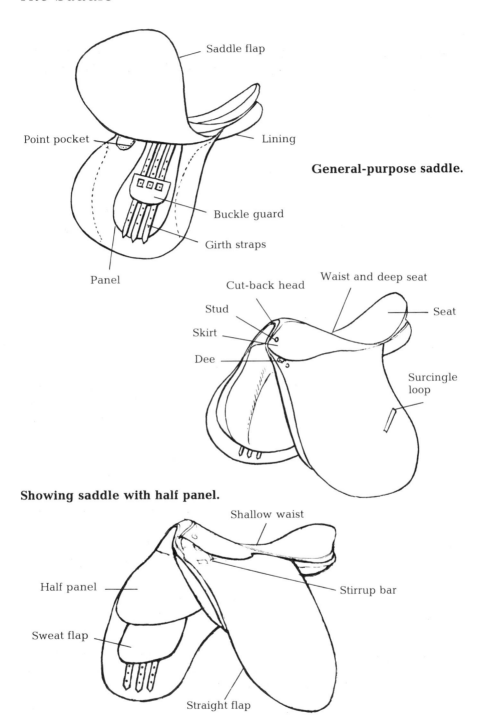

Saddle flap

Point pocket

Lining

General-purpose saddle.

Buckle guard

Girth straps

Panel

Cut-back head

Waist and deep seat

Stud

Seat

Skirt

Dee

Surcingle loop

Showing saddle with half panel.

Shallow waist

Half panel

Stirrup bar

Sweat flap

Straight flap

Racing

This is a lightweight saddle with a sloping head and very forward-cut flaps. Exercise racing saddles are built rather more substantially, although the design is similar.

Polo

This saddle may have a reinforced pommel. It is built with a short panel, extra long sweat flaps, and no knee or thigh rolls.

Pony Club

This saddle has the name 'Pony Club' stamped on it. It has a short panel with a good central-position seat, and no knee or thigh rolls.

ACCESSORIES

Girth

The following types can be used:

LEATHER GIRTHS, if well cared for, last much longer than any other type. The main types are: Three-fold, Balding and Atherstone. The latter two are shaped so that there is less risk of causing girth galls.

SHORT GIRTHS OF LEATHER OR MAN-MADE FABRIC suit dressage and jumping saddles with long girth straps.

NYLON is a good general-purpose material, which is easy to wash. Care should be taken that the girth does not get twisted.

STRING is similar to nylon but of harsher texture.

LAMPWICK is a soft comfortable girth, but does not stand up so well to hard wear.

Nylon, string and lampwick are inclined to shrink when washed, and they stretch when first put on. They need adjustment later.

WEBBING is generally preferred for racing, and by some riders for eventing. It is less restricting than leather. Two girths should always be used, as one can break without warning under strain.

WHITE TUBULAR WEBBING SHOW GIRTHS can be used on hacks and ponies. A piece of pimply rubber underneath makes them less likely to work forward – which can easily happen with a pony.
LEATHER OR WEBBING GIRTHS WITH ELASTIC INSERTS at the buckle ends are more often seen on racehorses and eventers. They are less restrictive to a horse when he is galloping than the conventional girth. The elastic needs regular checking for stretch and wear.
ELASTIC GIRTHS, which are sometimes used for racing, require careful adjustment. Sweat rots them in time.

Stirrup Leathers

These should be made of the best-quality leather. They should be chosen to suit the size and weight of the rider. It is dangerous to put a heavy leather on a lighter stirrup iron because if the rider falls the iron will not easily be freed from his foot. Lightweight leathers are often more comfortable for the rider and easier to handle. For racing, hunting, eventing and jumping, buffalo or rawhide leathers are the most suitable as they are less likely to break.

Extending Leather

This is useful for riders who have difficulty in mounting. Fitted on the near side of the saddle, it consists of a hook at the base of the buckle, and a slot attachment on the stirrup leather. The two are connected by a strong piece of tubular web. When open, the length of the leather is increased by 16 to 20cms (6 to 8ins) and allows for easier mounting. After the rider has mounted, the slot is put over the hook and the leather is then its normal length. Care must be taken to match up the two leathers so that they are level when in use. The webbing usually wears out more quickly than the leather, and should be regularly checked.

Stirrup Irons

Materials used are:
STAINLESS STEEL, which is the best.

COMPOSITE, which is satisfactory.

NICKEL, which is dangerous, as it bends and breaks. It can be recognised by its yellow colour. It requires regular polishing to stay bright.

The normal basic pattern stirrup iron is suitable for all purposes. The important factor is that the stirrup should be of suitable weight and size.

With the foot in the stirrup, there should be a 1.2cm (½in) clearance on either side. In the event of a fall, a too light stirrup and/or small stirrup may jam on the foot. Conversely, too large a stirrup can permit the rider's foot to slip right through. The correct size and weight of iron are therefore important, and should always be checked by the rider and/or attendant.

Alternative designs of stirrups are:
THE BENT TOP IRON. This is designed for the rider who keeps his foot well forward in the stirrup. Fitted so that it slopes forward, it removes pressure from the front of the leg. Fitting sloping backwards the reverse action occurs. The stirrup leather is placed through the iron with the curve away from the leather.

KOURNAKOFF. The eye of the iron is offset to the inside, and the sides slope forward with the tread sloped upwards. This helps to keep the heel lower than the toe, and the knee to be tight, with the lower leg off the horse. As it does not encourage an effective position of the rider's lower leg, it cannot be recommended. If it is used, however, it is essential to put the irons on correctly, and it is advisable to mark the left and the right.

SAFETY IRONS. These have a thick rubber band replacing the metal on one side of the iron. The band should always be to the outside. A leather loop fitted to the bottom of the iron helps to hold the rubber band and to prevent its being lost if it comes off the top hook. As the weight is uneven, these stirrups do not hang straight, but they are much safer than standard irons, and as such are advisable for young children.

The Saddle

RACING IRONS. These are usually made of lightweight stainless steel or aluminium. Because of their lightness they are not easily dislodged during a fall and are not suitable for general use.

Treads. Rubber or plastic treads are used to help the rider maintain his foot position. They are also warmer to the foot than metal.

BUYING AND FITTING SADDLES

Buying

Always buy the best that you can afford made by a reputable saddler. Good saddles, well looked after, last for years and retain their secondhand value. A cheap saddle may *look* suitable, but it has a limited life; trouble can be expected from the tree. The leather of the girth straps, saddle flaps, and seat may rapidly show signs of wear. A good secondhand saddle is usually a better buy than a cheaper new one, as long as the tree is undamaged.

If you are buying for a riding school, remember that rigid tree saddles are stronger and stand up to hard wear and heavyweights better than spring tree saddles. They are also likely to be less expensive. A wide-seated saddle, cut generously to spread the rider's weight, is kinder to the horse's back. The general-purpose type is preferable.

When buying for private use, many people prefer a spring tree saddle as it is more comfortable for the rider and gives a better feel of the horse's movement; also the seat aids are more directly felt by the horse.

Before deciding on a saddle, it is essential to ensure that it fits both the horse and the rider, and suits the latter. For the average rider, a general-purpose saddle is the most practical.

Fitting

A good saddler, who is a member of the Master Saddlers

Association, should always be happy to come out and fit a new saddle. He can then advise as to whether the tree is the correct shape and width, and can often adjust the panel-stuffing on the spot.

When you are having a saddle fitted, remember that the outline of a horse's back can change according to his management and work, and that the padding of a new saddle flattens during use. It may therefore have to be set up (padded up) by the saddler.

A good fitting and a comfortable saddle is essential if a horse is to perform well and avoid such problems as pressure and girth galls. A badly fitting saddle can be a cause of poor performance.

Procedure for Examining a Saddle

☐ Test the tree for signs of breakage or distortion (see below).

☐ Up-end the saddle and examine the underneath for any unevenness of padding or outline.

☐ Place the saddle on the saddle horse and check that the padding is level and even, both from behind and in front.

☐ Make sure that the gullet is wide enough – 6.3 to 7.5cms (2$^1/_2$ to 3ins) – so that there can be no pressure close to or on the spinal vertebrae. This must be checked again when the saddle is on the horse's back.

☐ To avoid marking the leather, a stable rubber should be placed on the horse's back under the saddle. To avoid marking the saddle flap, buckle guards should be fitted on the girth straps. The saddle should sit level and even, with no tilt either towards the cantle or the pommel. Either would effect the rider's position and make it difficult for him to stay in balance with his horse.

☐ The saddle should fit the horse with the weight evenly spread over the lumbar muscles, not the loins.

The Saddle

☐ It must not hamper the movement of the horse's shoulder. This can occur with a forward-cut jumping saddle.

☐ A rider, preferably the future owner or one of similar height and weight, should be legged up on to the horse. In both upright and jumping positions it should be possible to place four fingers under the pommel without feeling any pressure.

☐ There should be ample clearance under the cantle and along the gullet.

☐ When looked at from behind, it should be possible to see a clear channel of daylight.

To Test for a Damaged or Broken Tree

The Front Arch
The first indications of trouble are usually when the arch of the saddle widens and comes down on the withers. There may or may not be a squeaking or grating noise when the saddle is used; it is more likely to be heard with a heavy rider ● Place your hands on either wide of the pommel and try to widen and move the arch. Or hold the cantle and grip the pommel firmly between your knees. Any movement or clicking sound indicates damage.

The Waist
Rigid Tree:
Place the pommel against the stomach and, holding the cantle with both hands try to press it upwards and towards the pommel. A movement in the waist indicates a break or crack. If the tree is seriously damaged, the rough edge can usually be felt when the gullet is examined. Damage can occur either on both sides of the tree or on one side only.

Spring Tree
There should be some give in the seat of a spring tree saddle, but when it is tested as for a rigid tree it should

spring firmly back into place. A weak or broken tree feels slack and without spring.

It can be difficult for an inexperienced person to detect damage in a saddle with a spring tree. If you are in doubt, ask a saddler for advice.

Damage to a saddle caused by careless mounting by the rider can be observed by putting the saddle on a saddle horse and checking if there is a twist and/or if the saddle does not sit evenly.

Cantle
This should feel rigid. Any movement indicates damage.

Points
As these are the continuations of the front arch, they can be tested in a similar manner to that of the arch. Some saddles have flexible points, which should not be confused with damaged points. If the damage is below the stirrup bar, it is possible to see it.

To Measure a Horse's Back for a New Saddle
☐ Obtain a piece of soft lead or flexible wire: e.g. a coat hanger about 46cms (18ins) long.

☐ Place this just behind, and at right angles to, the horse's withers – in the position where the saddle would rest. Shape it into the required outline, then trace round it on a large sheet of paper.

☐ The next measurement should be taken about 23cms (9ins) further back and similarly traced.

☐ A third outline should be taken from the top of the withers along the spine.

☐ When ordering a saddle, it is helpful to give the rider's height, weight and length from crutch to knee.

Horses with Problem Conformation
The following are problems which need special attention in the fitting of saddles:

HIGH WITHERS. A narrow tree is necessary, well padded

Lead or wire for
measuring withers.

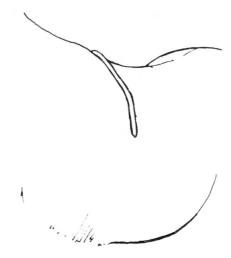

Measuring withers for the
saddle tree.

at the withers, and preferably 'cut back'. The saddle may have to be set up at the rear to give a level seat.

STRAIGHT SHOULDER. The saddle is likely to work forward, with a possible risk of girth galls. This is more likely if the horse is at grass and has a big belly. The rider feels insecure. The saddle needs careful padding to encourage it to stay back. A point strap can be fixed (see below).

FLAT SIDES. These encourage the saddle to slip back, which can be a problem when horses become fit. Careful padding of the saddle and the use of a breastplate should resolve the problem.

FAT PONIES WITH LOW WITHERS. The only satisfactory solution is to use a crupper. A point strap can also be fixed to the points of the tree, and the girth attached to this and to the first of the girth straps. This may help prevent the saddle sliding forward over the withers and on to the neck.

Typical Examples of Ill-fitting Saddles
☐ *Too much padding.* This causes the saddle to rock, with a risk of saddle sores, particularly on either side of the backbone to the rear of the saddle.

☐ *Too wide in the pommel.* This causes sores on the top of the withers and possible damage to the spine.

☐ *Points of the saddle too long.* This causes undue pressure on either side of the withers.

☐ *Uneven padding or a twisted tree.* This results in a crooked rider, uneven weight distribution, and the development of pressure and friction sores. It may also damage the muscles of the back.

☐ *A crooked rider* (see above) can also cause uneven muscle development of the horse's back, thus aggravating the crookedness.

Side-Saddles

TREE AND CONSTRUCTION. Most side-saddles used today are of pre-1939 construction. The tree is wooden, reinforced with metal, and with the top pommel built into it. The tree makes it heavy, and because of the shape and angle of the pommel or horn, it is easily damaged. Well-known makes of saddle are Owen, Champion & Wilts, Mayhew and Whippy, but unfortunately the makers no longer exist, having been closed down or bought up by larger concerns.

THE SEAT should be compact and flat, with the off side slightly set up to prevent the rider's seat from slipping over. A doeskin-covered seat gives more grip than a smooth leather seat ● The POMMELS or HORNS are spaced wide apart. The angle of the lower pommel or leaping head can be adjusted by tightening the horn pin. On some saddles, an alternative screw-in socket is provided. The adjustment is necessary according to the build of the rider, and whether she is riding on the flat or jumping. On some saddles, a small leather strap secures the pommel at the required angle ● The UNDERNEATH LINING should be of linen or serge, which is more comfortable for the horse, and less likely to cause a saddle rub. New saddles may have a leather lining ● If small round holes can be seen in the leatherwork, it is a sign that the tree may have been attacked by woodworm or small spiders ● When storing a saddle, cover it with fresh newspaper, as the printers' ink will deter the insects.

Buying a Side-Saddle

☐ Before buying a secondhand saddle it is advisable to have it checked over by a saddler experienced in this type of work. Repairs can be expensive, and in some cases the saddle may not be worth buying.

☐ Modern or post-war saddles are usually built on a tree of laminated wood, and are of simpler design. The tree is both stronger and much lighter: the saddle weighing around 5.5kg (12lbs). Older saddles weigh between 10kg (22lbs) and 12kg (26lbs).

☐ Before buying a saddle, make sure that it fits the horse. A good saddler can adjust the underneath padding as necessary. He may also be able to alter the padding and the set of the pommels to help the rider. If the saddle is made for a tall person it can never be altered sufficiently to enable a short rider to sit correctly. The reverse also applies.

Stirrup Attachment

All manufacturers of side-saddles had their own patented stirrup attachment, with the leather fitting made to match. The essential feature was a quick-release mechanism. Some of these can be difficult to manage if the user is inexperienced with a particular make ● They should all be kept well oiled.

Stirrup Leather and Iron

These have the necessary fitting at one end, with a metal hook attached at the other. The hook is put through the enlarged eye of the side-saddle iron, and then hooked back on itself. A leather sleeve slips down to cover the adjustable fastening ● The stirrup iron must be big enough for the rider's foot: the heavier the better ● A specially designed collapsible safety iron can sometimes be bought secondhand – although with a quick-release attachment it should not be necessary. Such irons can also be unreliable.

Girth and Balance Strap

The girth is usually of the three-fold leather or Atherstone type. Lampwick is suitable for showing ● The girth is first buckled on the near side ● The leather balance strap is fastened on the near side of the saddle, either with a buckle or strap, according to the make of the saddle. It is attached to the back of the saddle on the off side, and helps to keep the saddle steady. Nowadays, short balance straps are often used, sewn to the girth on the off side and then fastened to the saddle. Opinion is divided as to which is the most efficient ● On some saddles with girths which buckle under the off-side flap, there is a strap to hold down the flap. The flap strap is sewn to the bottom of the near-side saddle flap, and is fastened with buckles under the horse's belly. A hook on the near-side flap then fastens it to the strap ● The girths of many saddles are now fastened to girth straps on the outside of the off-side flap, which make the extra strap redundant.

CHAPTER 2
Bridles

Leatherwork must be of a suitable size and weight. Show and dressage bridles can be of lightweight leather. Bridles for hunting, eventing, show jumping and riding-school work should be of a heavier type.

Parts of a Snaffle Bridle
☐ Headpiece and throat lash.

☐ Browband.

☐ Cheek pieces.

☐ Noseband, either attached or with a cavesson: i.e. with separate headpiece.

☐ Reins.

☐ Snaffle bit.

Parts of a Double Bridle
☐ Headpiece and throat lash.

☐ Browband.

☐ Cheek pieces.

☐ Noseband. (See note under snaffle bridle, above.)

☐ Bridoon headpiece.

☐ Bridoon cheek piece.

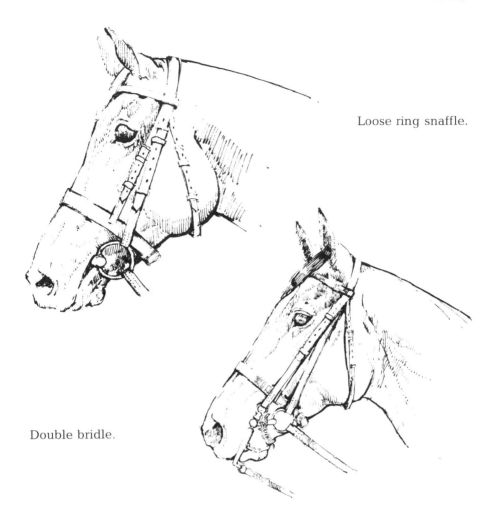

Loose ring snaffle.

Double bridle.

- [ ] Bridoon rein, often thinner than a snaffle rein. It may be laced, plaited or covered with rubber.
- [ ] Curb rein (thinner than the bridoon rein).
- [ ] Bridoon.
- [ ] Bit (curb).
- [ ] Curb chain (metal or leather).
- [ ] Lip strap (optional). Some bits do not have the necessary 'Ds'.

Parts of a Pelham

☐ Headpiece.

☐ Browband.

☐ Cheek pieces.

☐ Noseband. (See note under snaffle bridle.)

☐ Bridoon rein and curb rein as for double bridle above. Or Pelham rounding and one rein.

☐ Pelham bit.

☐ Curb chain.

☐ Lip strap.

REINS

Reins should be chosen according to intended use. A full size rein should be 1.5m (5ft) in length: i.e. the longest strip which can be cut from a hide. Reins for show jumping or flat racing – when a shorter hold is taken – can be 1.4m (4½ft). Pony reins can be 1.3m (4ft 3ins) or shorter.

Types of Rein

LEATHER REINS can be plain, plaited, laced or rubber-covered. The latter when used for steeplechasing or eventing should have enough plain leather at the buckle end to enable them to be knotted. If the rider should slip the reins to the buckle end, the strain can be taken on the knot, not the buckle.

OTHER MATERIALS are webbing, linen, plaited cotton and nylon. These are all popular for jumping. Some have leather slots stitched every 13 to 16cms (5 to 6ins) to provide a more secure hold.

MAN-MADE FIBRE AND COTTON. This is a cheap and efficient replacement for leather. For the average horse it is comfortable, but the texture can be harsh, and horses with sensitive skins may react adversely. As this material is easy to clean it is an acceptable means of saving many hours otherwise taken up by the care of leather. It can be recommended for schooling and hacking, as it lasts longer and is stronger than inferior or neglected leather.

Good-quality leather, well cared for, remains the first preference.

Buckles should be of good-quality metal.

FITTING A BRIDLE

When the bridle is on the horse, check the following points:
- ☐ The fit of the browband. This must be comfortable. If it is too tight it will pinch the ears; if too loose, the headpiece may slip back causing the browband to look untidy.

- ☐ The headpiece and cheek pieces should be an even height on both sides, and preferably of such a length that the buckles lie just above eye level.

- ☐ The snaffle bit should be adjusted so as to wrinkle slightly the corners of the horse's mouth and not to protrude more than 0.5cm or ¼in on each side. The horse's mouth should be opened to make sure that the bit is high enough in his mouth to clear the tushes. The bit should be pulled out straight to measure its width.

- ☐ The throat lash should be buckled so that it is possible to place a hand between the leather and the horse's jaw *when the head is flexed.* Some thick-jowled horses may need it looser than this.

- ☐ The cavesson noseband should be fitted two finger breadths of 2.5cms (1in) below the cheek bone. When it is fastened at the back, allow two fingers' width between the jaw and the leather. During training it may, if necessary, be tightened.

- ☐ The reins should have about 43 to 51cms (15 to 20ins) spare when the rider is holding them. They must never be so long that the slack part can be looped over the rider's foot. They should be buckled together at the ends.

Fitting a Double Bridle

The fit of the browband, headpiece, throat lash and noseband should be similar to that of a snaffle bridle.

☐ The bridoon bit should be fitted on a separate headpiece, which should buckle on the off side a little below the buckle of the main headpiece, at a height which will slightly wrinkle the horse's lips.

☐ The bit should lie below the bridoon so that both can act independently.

☐ The curb chain should be hooked on the off side of the bit, so that when twisted clockwise to the right the lip strap ring will hang down. The flat ring of the curb chain should be put on the near-side hook with the thumb nail down. The selected link should be taken up and also attached with thumb nail down and maintaining the twist to the right. If it is shortened more than three links, take up an equal number on both sides ● The end links of a leather-covered chain should be put on in a similar manner ● If no links need to be taken up, the curb chain should be put on the hook with the thumb uppermost.

☐ The curb chain should lie flat in the chin groove, and remain flat when the cheeks of the bit are drawn back. There must be no risk of rubbing the horse on this very sensitive part of the jaw. A modern single-link curb chain cannot be thus adjusted, as the links will not stay flat. Double link or leather curb chains are preferable. The curb chain must never be fitted through the rings of the bridoon. Its action must be quite independent of the bridoon.

☐ The lip strap should be put through the loose ring of the curb chain and buckled on the near side. It is decorative, rather than functional. If used, there is less danger of losing a curb chain when the bridle is being carried.

☐ A bridoon rein may be slightly shorter than that of a snaffle bridle. If so, the bit rein should be 20 to 30cms (8 to 12ins) longer than the bridoon rein.

Fitting a Pelham Bridle

This is fitted so that the bit lies close up against the corners of the lips without wrinkling them. The curb chain, when fitted, should lie in the curb groove. The curb chain should be hooked on as for a double bridle and should have a lip strap. The chain can be placed through the top ring of the Pelham, which prevents any friction from the curb hook on the sides of the horse's face. Alternatively, it can go directly from hook to hook. If the upper cheek of the Pelham is too long, the action of the curb chain will be too high up (see below).

Fitting a Kimblewick

This is fitted in a similar manner to a Pelham. The correct fitting of the curb chain depends on the length of the horse's jaw. With many horses, the chain lies above the chin groove and its pressure is felt on sensitive bone.

NB: *Curb chain hooks must open outwards*, away from the horse's face.

NOSEBANDS

Drop Noseband

This is used to prevent a horse opening his mouth so wide that he can evade the action of the bit.

Correct fitting is essential. If it is fitted too low, it interferes with the horse's breathing and can cause distress ● The front of the noseband should lie on the bony part of the nose ● The strap at the back should drop down to be fastened below the snaffle bit ● The noseband should allow the horse to flex and move his jaw, but should prevent him from opening his mouth wide.

Rings which connect the front nosepiece to the back strap have small hooks which, when the leather is firmly stitched, hold up the front nosepiece and prevent it dropping down. Alternatively, short leather straps can be attached from the nosepiece to the headpiece. Some nosebands have adjustable fronts to ensure a better fit over the nose.

Common Faults in Manufacture
- The front strap is too long, which makes fitting difficult, and the horse's face and lips can get pinched.
- The buckle end of the back strap is too long, making adjustment difficult. The buckle end should be short and the strap end long.
- The front strap is not on fixed rings, and therefore drops down.
- The headpiece is too long, resulting in an untidy and unnecessary length of strap.

The Grakle, Figure-of-Eight or Cross-over Noseband
This is made of lighter-weight leather than a drop noseband. Its action is similar, but it is also effective in preventing a horse from crossing his jaw, as it acts over a wider area of the head. It is also less likely to affect the horse's breathing. It acts from a headpiece, which ends immediately above the horse's cheekbone or just below. Two straps cross over the bridge of the nose, where they are stitched together and are usually padded underneath. They then pass round the horse's nose, and are buckled above and below the bit. They can be adjusted as required, but must allow some freedom to the mouth, although not so loosely that the lower strap drops down under the horse's chin. A small adjustable strap can also prevent this.

The Flash Noseband
This is a cavesson noseband on to which a light strap is sewn, or is put through a small loop on the front of the cavesson section ● The strap fastens below the bit, and acts

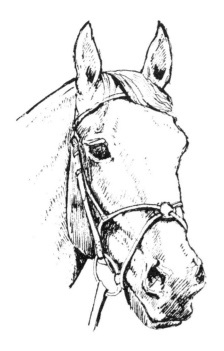

Grakle noseband.   Flash noseband.

in a similar way to a drop noseband. It is easier to fit than a drop, and is generally more comfortable for the horse.

The Kineton Noseband
This may help in the control of a strong horse. It acts by transferring some of the rein pressure from the mouth to the bridge of the nose. Note that it can also restrict breathing ● It consists of two metal loops, one end of which is attached to a short, adjustable, centre strap, the other to a long head-piece ● It is worn with a snaffle bit ● The metal hoops fit round the mouthpiece between the bit ring and the horse's face ● The centre strap should rest on the bony part of the horse's nose.

CHAPTER 3
Other Saddlery

MARTINGALES

In theory, the educated rider on a well-schooled horse should not need auxiliary aids such as martingales. There are occasions, however, when they can be used with benefit, to prevent the horse or pony putting his head above the angle of control, and so to help the rider to manage his horse as well as to improve the safety factor.

Running Martingale
The running martingale consists of a thin neck strap buckled on the near side and with a loop at the bottom. A wide strap is put through the loop. At one end it has an adjustable loop through which the girth is threaded. At the other end it is divided into two, each end having a ring through which the reins are threaded.

This acts via the reins and should be adjusted so that it only comes into action when the horse puts his head up. It also can be used by a novice or unbalanced rider who carries his hands too high, as this ensures that the action of the rein is kept lower, which is less likely to upset the horse.

A rough guide to fitting is to hold both the ring ends of the martingale together and to draw them towards the withers when the loop end is through the girth. If they reach the withers, the fit is loose. When adjusted too tightly they can cause insensitive hands to damage a horse's jaw — as they have a very severe action with strong downward pressure on the bars of the mouth.

As a running martingale affects the rein contact with the horse's mouth, two reins may be used, with the martingale attached to the bottom rein, thus leaving the other rein free to maintain direct contact. When attaching the reins: to ensure that they can slide smoothly through the rings, stand on the near side, hold the rings up with the right hand, and thread each rein through separately. Then buckle the reins together.

Reins not sewn on to the bit should have rubber or leather stops to prevent the martingale rings catching on the fastenings. The stops will also be necessary if a martingale is used on the curb rein of a double bridle or Pelham on which the bit rings are smaller than the martingale rings. This practice is not recommended. A running martingale on a bridoon rein is more effective and less severe.

A strong rubber ring or stop should also be used to secure the neck strap to the martingale.

The girth strap loop should have two keepers which should be adjusted to hold the loop flat.

The running martingale detracts from the correct use of the open rein.

Standing Martingale

A standing martingale prevents the horse from putting, or throwing, his head up above the angle of control: a bad habit which can result in the rider receiving a bang on his nose.

The martingale is secured to the neck strap and girth in a similar manner to the running martingale, but it is then attached directly to a cavesson noseband. It should never be attached to a drop noseband.

It is adjustable either:
- At the girth.
- By a buckle under the neck.
- At the noseband.

When the horse's head is in a normal position, it should be possible to push the martingale up into the horse's gullet. It should not be fitted so tight that it exerts continual pressure, as this will encourage the horse to lean up against it. It also restricts a horse's action, particularly over a jump.

Combined Martingale
This is a combination of a standing and running martingale and has the action of both. It is more often used for show jumping.

Bib Martingale
This is similar to a running martingale, but with a centre piece of leather between the two rings. It can be used on an excitable or overbent horse who is likely to catch his teeth in the strap or ring of an ordinary running martingale. It is more restrictive, as an opening rein cannot be used.

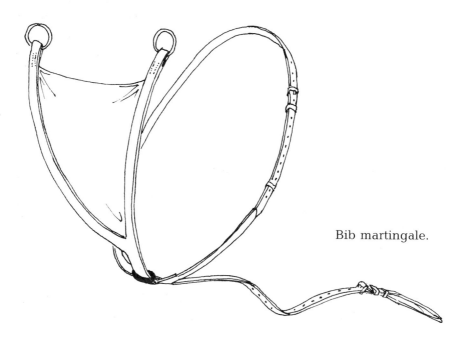

Bib martingale.

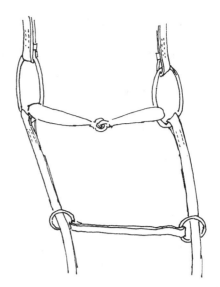

Irish martingale with stitched reins.

Irish Martingale

This consists of a short leather strap about 10 to 12cms (4 to 5ins) long, with a ring at either end. The reins are threaded through the rings, and if the reins are not sewn on, stops must be used. It is positioned under the horse's neck. In the event of a fall, it helps to prevent the reins going over the horse's head. It is more generally used on racehorses. It can also help a horse who shakes his head and gets the reins over his head when being ridden. It can adjust the angle of the rein contact down if the hands are too high.

BREASTPLATE

This is used to prevent the saddle slipping back – usually on horses who are very fit or on those whose conformation fails to prevent the saddle from slipping back (i.e. flat sided or herring gutted horses). It is also used when hunting in very hilly country.

There are two types of breastplate:

1. A LEATHER NECK STRAP is attached first to the girth by a leather strap and then to the 'Ds' of the saddle by two

narrow leather straps on either side of the withers. The neck strap has buckles on both sides, so that it can be evenly adjusted. It should fit comfortably and not be tight around the neck.

If a martingale is used, a short attachment can be added, either in the design of a running or standing martingale. This can be buckled to the centre ring of the neck strap and then put on to the reins or the noseband as required. This centre ring should have a leather 'safe' or protecting pad to avoid any rubbing of the horse.

2. AN 'AINTREE BREASTGIRTH', which is more often used on racehorses or eventers. It consists of a band of webbing or wide elastic which is passed round the horse's chest and attached to the girth on either side by adjustable leather loops. Another strap is passed over the horse's withers, which prevents the breast girth from dropping down. The breast girth must be carefully fitted so that neck movement and the windpipe are not affected.

SPECIAL GIRTHS

Surcingle or Overgirth

This is essential equipment for racing and eventing, but is also used in show jumping. It is a high-quality webbing strap, long enough to fit over the top of a saddle and weight cloth. It helps to hold everything in place, and acts as an extra girth in an emergency. Some may have a small but very strong elastic inset, which makes for easier fitting.

Foregirth

This has a metal arch positioned in front of the saddle to stop it slipping forward. It is attached to a surcingle, which must be buckled up tightly before the saddle is put on. It is used particularly in dressage to ensure that the saddle does not come too far forward, thus putting the rider's weight on to the shoulders.

WEIGHT CLOTH

This is necessary when a rider has to carry weight to conform to competition rules: e.g. in racing, eventing, and show jumping. It consists of a strong linen or man-made fibre saddle cloth secured to the saddle by leather straps, and with stitched pockets for holding lead. The pockets can be placed in front of the saddle – on the shoulders, or behind the saddle flaps and against the horse's ribs. When fitting a leaded weight cloth, care must be taken that it does not press down on the withers, or interfere with the rider's position.

NUMNAHS

These are protective pads worn under a saddle to add to the horse's comfort and to protect his back from friction and pressure. They are especially valuable:

- ☐ When first riding the horse after a long rest.
- ☐ When riding for a long period of time with the rider's weight continually on the horse's back.
- ☐ With learners, who find it difficult to sit quietly and in balance, particularly if they are of heavy build.
- ☐ With experienced or novice riders who do not sit straight and square in the saddle. The uneven distribution of weight can encourage the saddle to rock, and creates additional friction.
- ☐ With a modern saddle which has a spring tree, narrow waist and deep seat, and which concentrates pressure over a smaller area.
- ☐ When the shape of a horse's back changes. A numnah will then make the saddle fit more comfortably. This should only be a temporary measure, as the stuffing of the saddle has to be altered.
- ☐ When jumping. A numnah under the saddle adds to the horse's comfort and encourages him to jump with a rounded back.

NB. The saddle should fit the horse's back before the

numnah is put on. Except in emergencies, it should not be put on to make a badly fitting saddle usable.

Types of Numnah

SHEARED SHEEPSKIN is a natural fibre which absorbs sweat. It can be washed, but afterwards the leather side requires treating to keep it soft. This type of numnah is expensive.

NYLON 'SHEEPSKIN' is cheaper and not so absorbent, but it is very easy to wash and quick to dry.

LINEN or good-quality COTTON with a PLASTIC FOAM LINING can be satisfactory and is sweat-absorbent.

PLAIN RUBBER FOAM is cheap and easily cut to shape, but unless covered with cotton or linen, it does not wear well and tends to draw the horse's back, causing sweating and ruffling of the hair. Many new synthetic materials are now on the market.

A WOOLLEN BLANKET folded in four makes an effective back protector should a saddle have insufficient padding.

Natural fibres – wool, linen, cotton – are the best choice as some horses are allergic to man-made fibres. Numnahs are best washed with soap, as again some horses are allergic to detergents. Numnahs must be kept very clean – even if it means daily washing.

Numnahs are secured in place by:
- ☐ Light leather straps and buckles.
- ☐ Nylon loops, which fit round the girth straps.
- ☐ Velcro straps.
- ☐ Strong elastic.
- ☐ Leather loops, which are the most satisfactory type for hard or competition work.

WITHER PADS

These can be of woollen cloth or foam rubber. They are

used under the front arch of a saddle, which would otherwise press on the horse's withers. They should be considered an emergency remedy, as their use often upsets the balance of the saddle and encourages the rider's seat to slip back. The saddle should be restuffed to make the use of such pads unnecessary ● They can be used under stable rollers and breaking rollers.

CRUPPER

This is usually worn by small, fat ponies or donkeys to prevent the saddle or roller from slipping forward.

The crupper consists of an adjustable leather strap put through a metal ring or 'D' on the cantle of the saddle. The other end of the strap is a padded and rounded leather loop, through which the tail is placed. This may or may not have a separate fastening. When fitting the crupper, place it over the tail first, well up under the dock. Then connect it to the saddle and adjust it to a comfortable length. Care should be taken when first fitting, as ponies not used to a crupper may buck or kick. If they are worn frequently, the skin under the tail may become sore, and this area should be regularly examined. The crupper loop must be kept soft and supple.

GRASS REINS

These are adjustable narrow leather, nylon or cord reins which are attached round the girth straps or clipped to the saddle 'Ds'. They are then crossed over the withers and attached to the bit rings, or they may be fitted through the browband loops and down to the bit. They are used to prevent a pony from putting his head down to eat, thus pulling off a small rider. They also help to control a pony who bucks. It may be necessary to fit a crupper to prevent the saddle from being pulled forward.

NECK STRAP

This is a strap which is fastened round the horse's neck and buckled on the near side. It can be a stirrup leather. It is used (a) to give unbalanced novice riders something to hold on to rather than the reins, and (b) to help more experienced riders on young or fresh horses who might buck. If required, it can be attached to the front 'Ds' of the saddle and/or to the girth between the front legs.

HEADCOLLAR

A good-quality headcollar is an expensive item because of the amount of leather and stitching involved. Various designs are available: brass-mounted, with buckles on both sides, being the smartest (as well as the most expensive). A cheaper headcollar with galvanised or tin fittings and less stitching is perfectly adequate; in many cases the stitching is now replaced by rivets. The front may unbuckle, which makes it easier when brushing the face and when putting on a bridle. Nylon headcollars are a cheap and suitable substitute for leather but they can be dangerous as the nylon is virtually unbreakable.

A headcollar should be fitted so that the noseband lies 5cms (2ins) below the cheek bones and allows a hand to be held between the leather and the jaw bones. Tight headcollars cause discomfort and result in sore patches.

Foal slips should be made of leather, with adjustable buckles on the headpiece and noseband to allow for growing. Nylon foal slips are unsafe. A 16cm (6in) strip of leather, which a hand can hold, should be attached to the back of the noseband.

Ropes

These are made of:
HEAVY JUTE, which is strong and stands most wear.
COLOURED COTTON, which is attractive but can snap.
NYLON, which is strong but which should be discarded

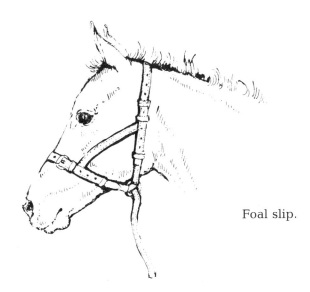

Foal slip.

when frayed; a frayed rope, when knotted, can be impossible to untie.

PLAITED BINDER TWINE. This, if carefully plaited, with no loose ends or knots, is effective and is also easily and cheaply replaced.

Ropes are made with an eye, or are fitted with a spring hook which when attached to the headcollar should face away from the horse's chin and towards the neck. On occasions, spring hooks have been known to catch in a horse's face.

HALTERS

These are made of webbing or rope, and usually have the rope as an integral part of the halter. The 'Yorkshire' type of *webbing halter* is very strong and has a string throat lash which prevents the halter from being pulled over the head. *Rope halters* are adjustable and can be altered to fit any size of head.

It is important to ensure that the nose section of the halter cannot pull tight and panic the horse. After fitting, a knot should be tied by putting the head rope round the noseband

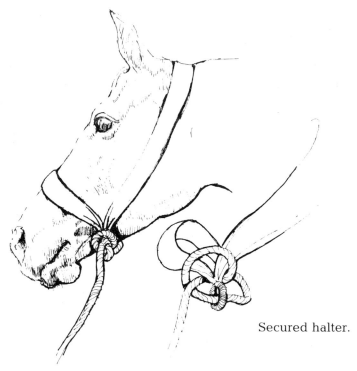

Secured halter.

and pulling it back through the loop. This prevents the halter from tightening and also from working loose.

LUNGEING EQUIPMENT

Cavesson
The modern cavesson is lightweight and is made of either leather or man-made fibre. It must be well padded in the nose area, so that pressure will not cause a sore. There are two patterns:

The nose piece is made like a drop noseband with the back straps attached to rings, so that they can be fitted either above or below the bit.
The nose piece is made like a cavesson noseband, and fits round the nose above the bit.

Both patterns have a jointed metal plate on the front of the noseband with a central swivel-mounted ring. They

44

may also have small rings on either side. They should be firmly fastened or they will cause rubbing on the front of the nose.

A securing strap is set about halfway down the headpiece. This passes over the cheek bones and fastens on the near side. It holds the cavesson in place and must be firmly fastened. If it is set too high, its firm hold causes discomfort and affects the horse's ability to flex at the poll.

Lunge Roller or Pad

This is made of leather, man-made fibre or strong reinforced webbing approximately 10cms (4ins) wide, and should be well padded over the back. It can be shaped in the elbow area to avoid rubbing the horse's sides. It should have two buckles on either side to ensure that when the roller is fitted the rings on either side are at the same height. It is also safer to have two buckles when dealing with a young horse who may play up as the buckles are tightened.

Rings should be fixed on to the roller:
☐ On the front and back of the top.
☐ Approximately 5 cms (2ins) below the top on either side.
☐ On the girth section near the buckles.
☐ Underneath of the girth.
☐ 'Ds' should be fixed as for a rug roller, to hold the breastplate.

If required, a pad may be put under the roller. For a young horse, who may buck, the pad should be attached to the roller.

Breastplate

This is a leather or webbing strap placed round the chest and fastened to the lower rings or 'Ds' of the roller to prevent it from slipping back. For the lungeing of young horses it should always be used, even with side reins.

Side Reins

These are adjustable leather straps about 1.8m (6ft) long,

which run from the roller or saddle to the bit. They are used:

☐ To teach the young horse to accept the bit.
☐ To help to keep the horse straight, and if lungeing in a paddock to prevent him from snatching at a mouthful of grass.
☐ To increase control over a fresh or strong horse.
☐ To improve the trained horse's way of going.
☐ To teach a horse piaffe from the ground.
☐ To lunge a rider and so help to keep the horse in better balance and give the rider a better feel of the paces.

There are two types:

1. At one end the leather strap fits through the rings on the roller (or round the girth of a saddle), and returns to buckle on itself. To allow for adjustment, there should be at least twelve numbered holes. At the other end, strong spring clips facing outwards and away from the horse are clipped to the bit rings, or on occasion to the side rings of the cavesson.
2. Similar to (1), but with a loop to go round the roller or girth and an adjustable fastening in the middle.

Some side reins are made with rubber rings or strong elastic inserts. If the elastic becomes stretched, it must be replaced.

Some trainers prefer not to use side reins for lungeing, because they feel that the horse should feel free to adjust his head and neck position according to his natural balance. This applies particularly in the early stages.

When changing the rein or when the horse is not being worked, side reins should be unfastened and put over the withers or clipped to the side 'Ds'. Side reins should not be attached until the rider has mounted the horse and should be fitted with care. Whether training the horse, or when lungeing the rider, the side reins must never be fitted so tight that free forward movement is hampered. It is advisable to lunge a strange horse without side reins – or without loose ones – for a few minutes before fitting the side reins.

Lunge Reins

A lunge rein, unless for ponies, should not be less than 10 metres or 33 feet in length. It should have a loop at one end and an attachment to the cavesson at the other.

Materials for Reins
☐ Tubular or straight linen webbing.
☐ Nylon.
☐ Rope.
Webbing is strong but may be a little heavy. *Nylon* is strong but very light – this can make it difficult to handle, and even with gloves on it can cut into or burn the hand. *Rope* is strong, and lighter than webbing, but can be more difficult to handle and may burn the hand.

Cavesson Attachments for Lunge Reins
☐ Swivel joint with buckle or strong clip.
☐ Strong clip.
☐ Leather strap and buckle.
If the cavesson has a swivel it is not necessary to have a swivel on the buckle or clip, as this makes the attachments heavy for a young horse. When a horse is jumping on the lunge it is cumbersome and can bang his nose.

Lunge Whip

This should be carefully chosen. Most whips are now made of fibreglass, with a thin plaited thong about 2.4m (8ft) long, with a lash at the end. The whip must be well balanced, and not so heavy that it will be tiring and difficult to manipulate. It must be long enough for the lunger to influence the horse and, when necessary, to touch him with the lash. To give extra length, the short lash can be replaced by a long leather boot lace.

Crupper

The use of a crupper is optional. It can be a helpful extra discipline for an obstreperous young horse. It should be of leather, with a well padded dock piece. It should have a separate buckle for fastening round the dock.

When lungeing it is essential for the lunger to wear gloves and stout, sensible footwear.

LONG REINING

Equipment for this is similar to that for lungeing, but it includes two reins which are often lighter and shorter than a full lunge rein.

GADGETS

Gadgets are auxiliary aids which, by positive action, govern the position of the horse's head. In experienced hands they have their uses in the restraining of spoilt or 'nappy' horses. They can also be used, on veterinary advice, in the building up of back and hindquarter muscles after injury. In the hands of inexperienced riders they may produce more problems than they cure and can result in severe muscle strain. They have no place in the classical and systematic schooling of the horse.

Running or Draw Rein

This is the simplest and most commonly used auxiliary aid. It consists of a double-length rein made of leather, webbing or nylon, with a loop at either end. It may or may not have a buckle in the middle. It is fitted by passing the ends of the reins through the bit rings (from the outside to the inside) and back to the girth. The loops may go between the horse's front legs and through the girth, or be put through the girth on either side of the horse at the required height. The lower the rein the more effective and also more severe the action.

Market Harborough

This is a type of running martingale, and is the least severe of the auxiliary aids. The divided pieces of the martingale go through the rings of the bit. They either clip back on to 'Ds' stitched on the reins, or are attached by an adjustable buckle. When the horse's head is in a normal position it has no restrictive influence, but it comes into use if the horse raises or throws up his head. It can therefore be effective on headstrong horses.

Chambon

This is used for lungeing. It consists of a divided rein which goes from the girth through rings on a special fitting attached to the headpiece behind the horse's ears, and from there to the bit where it is attached by clips.

A horse wearing a chambon is worked on the lunge in a circle of 20 metres in a *slow* trot, and with the equipment loosely fitting until the horse is familiar with it. It is gradually tightened, so that the horse moves with a lowered head. He will then accept the restriction without worrying • Schooling time should start with two to three minutes on each rein, and should never exceed a total of twenty minutes • The horse should not be expected to move in a working trot. If this is demanded, it can only have the affect of forcing the horse on to his forehand • The horse should never be ridden in a chambon • In the hands of an expert, lungeing with the chambon can be beneficial, but unskilled use can easily cause damage.

There are various other types of gadget on the market, most of which, working on some form of lever principle, persuade the horse to lower his head and go in a rounder outline. Some gadgets can be attached to the tail: but it is worth remembering that the tail is an extension of the horse's spine. If the horse is not permitted to carry his tail in a natural manner, the use of the back muscles can be adversely affected and the muscles of the tail may suffer permanent damage.

CHAPTER 4
Bits

The purpose of a bit is to enable a rider to control and guide his horse. The success of this control also depends on the effectiveness of the rider's seat and leg aids. The bit functions by bringing pressure to bear on the horse's mouth and head, either by direct action of the bit or by the indirect action of the bridle. This action will be affected by the horse's mouth, the angle at which he carries his head, the height of the rider's hands, and the design and fit of the bit.

Structure of the Mouth
The horse has an upper and lower jaw, the comparative length of which varies in different breeds, and can affect both the action of the bit and that of the curb chain.

The parts of the lower jaw bone lying between the incisor teeth in the front and the molars at the back of the mouth are called 'the bars'. They are covered with a layer of skin and flesh containing nerves. In a young horse, this area is very sensitive, but can become deadened by rough use of the bit.

The top of the mouth is formed by the palate – a very sensitive area.

In stallions and geldings, *tushes* grow on either side of the jaw between the incisors and the molars. If present in mares they are usually rudimentary and barely visible. *Wolf teeth* may grow at the front, and to the side of the first molars.

They can cause bitting problems and should be removed.

The areas on which the bit and/or bridle act are:
- [ ] The corners of the mouth and lips.
- [ ] The bars of the mouth.
- [ ] The tongue.
- [ ] The roof of the mouth.
- [ ] The side of the face.
- [ ] The chin groove.
- [ ] The nose.
- [ ] The poll.

PROBLEMS IN THE MOUTH

Causes:
- [ ] Sharp molars.
- [ ] Wolf teeth.
- [ ] Sensitivity of the skin covering the bars of the mouth.
- [ ] The length of the jaw, or the position and size of the tushes.
- [ ] The shape of the jaw relative to the size of the tongue.
- [ ] A badly fitting or badly fitted bit.

If after inspection the problem does not appear to lie in the mouth, other possible causes are:
- [ ] Physical discomfort and/or pain caused by ill-fitting tack other than the bit.
- [ ] Pain from unsoundness in the back or legs.
- [ ] The hands of an insensitive or unbalanced rider.

If the horse has discomfort or pain in his mouth he may try to ease this by altering his head position and opening his mouth, which brings pressure to bear on a less sensitive surface: i.e. the corners of the mouth rather than the bars. If the latter become deadened because of insensitive treatment, then all too often the rider will seek a stronger bit and a more severe method of control. If mouth problems are encountered, the cause should first be investigated. In many cases, a change of bit to a milder type often solves the problem.

Types of Problem

- A too narrow bit pinches and rubs the corners of the mouth. A too wide bit runs through the mouth when one rein is pulled, and a joint may even go across the mouth and rest on the bars. If jointed, it may press on the roof of the mouth, when the rider has a less direct feel of the mouth.

- A horse with a shallow mouth space between the upper and lower jaws, or a thick tongue, may find a thick bit uncomfortable because of tongue pressure. The joint of the bit may press up into the roof of the mouth, and a bit which is too wide aggravates the problem. With such horses, make sure that the bit fits the mouth: i.e. that it only extends just to the outside of the lips. Use a tapered mouthpiece: i.e. thick at the ends and thinner towards the centre. Try a double-jointed or French snaffle, as the smooth centre plate should lie comfortably on top of the tongue and there is no nutcracker action.

- A horse with a normal mouth space and sensitive bars may find a thin mouthpiece sharp to the tongue, and uncomfortable on the bars. Use a thick-jointed or double-jointed mouthpiece. This can be of the German hollow mouth type – which is light – or it can be covered in rubber or leather.

- A horse can double back his tongue and try to put it over the bit. This may be due to discomfort, especially if the bit is relatively low in the mouth, when there will be excessive tongue pressure. A mullen mouth snaffle can be more comfortable, and if fixed high in the mouth it may also discourage or check the habit of tongue over bit. Alternatively, try a single or double-jointed snaffle fixed high in the mouth.

- A dry mouth is the sign of an insensitive mouth, and the horse is often very strong. He must be encouraged to salivate, and bits which stimulate this are leather and copper types, key ring snaffles, or a curb chain tied in the mouth below a jointed snaffle.

- A horse often tries to avoid the action or message from the bit by opening his mouth and/or crossing his jaw. Various nosebands can help this problem (see page 31).

CONSTRUCTION OF THE BIT

The mouthpiece of a bit can be made of metal, vulcanite, nylon, rubber or leather. The metals used are stainless steel, composition alloy, chromium-plated steel and nickel.

Types of Material
STAINLESS STEEL is the safest and best looking metal. The second choice is one of the named composition alloys.
CHROMIUM PLATED STEEL is safe, but the chrome has a limited life and flakes off, causing a roughened surface and exposing rusty steel.
PURE NICKEL BITS are still in common use, but they can be dangerous, as they snap without warning. Nickel is a soft metal which wears quickly. It is used in snaffles of the flat ring type, where the ring goes through the bit. It often wears, becomes sharp, and can rub a horse's mouth. The centre joint of such snaffles can wear through, at first causing discomfort, and then coming apart. The colour, depending on care, ranges from dull to bright yellow.
ALUMINIUM can be used if a light but strong bit is required, as in racing.
COPPER is a soft metal. It is suitable for *covering* steel mouthpieces, but where there is any strain, it should not be used on its own. Some horses are known to go well in copper-covered bits, as the taste of the metal can encourage salivation.
VULCANITE is rubber hardened by heat. It makes a thick, heavy mouthpiece, which is kind in action.
NYLON is very light but strong.
RUBBER makes a very soft but kind bit. It should always have an internal mouthpiece of linked steel.

RAWHIDE LEATHER or LEATHER STRIPS can be stitched over an internal mouthpiece of steel or copper wire.

Bit Fittings

At each end of the mouthpiece are the fittings to which the headpiece and reins are attached. They can be of various designs. Loose and flat ring snaffles allow a certain amount of movement of the bit within the rings. Eggbutt, D-shape and cheeked snaffles limit this movement. Examples of the different types are found in the following text.

TYPES OF BIT

There are five main types of bit or bridle, all of which have many variations. These are:

☐ The Snaffle.
☐ The Double.
☐ The Pelham.
☐ The Gag Snaffle.
☐ The Hackamore/Bitless Bridle.

Note There are restrictions on bits used in competitions governed by the FEI and the BHS. Illustrations of permitted bits can be found in the relevant rule book.

To Measure a Bit

Lay the bit flat and measure the distance between the inner sides of the bit rings or cheek.

Bits are made in sizes ranging from 9cms (3½ins) to 15cms (6ins), and go up in 0.5cm (¼in) to 1cm (½in) stages.

To Measure a Horse's Mouth

Hold up a piece of thick string in the mouth. Mark with your fingers where the sides of the corners of the lip occurs. Remove the string and measure between the marks. It can often be difficult to buy the exact width of bit required, particularly in the smaller sizes, and it may be necessary to approach several suppliers. Remember that the height of the horse will not reflect the size of the required bit. This will be governed by type and breeding.

THE ACTION OF THE SNAFFLE BIT

There are many variations of snaffle, but the main ones are:
☐ Solid mouthpiece with no joint.
☐ One joint with two arms.
☐ Two joints with two arms and a middle link, which encourages more play in the mouth and has no nutcracker action.

A straight bar or curved (mullen mouth) mouthpiece with no joint works on the lips and directly on to the bars of the mouth. If the tongue is large there is also considerable tongue pressure. If the tongue is small the bars will take more pressure.

With a single joint mouthpiece there is a nutcracker action when the joint closes. It also acts on the bars of the mouth and the lips, but there is less tongue pressure than with a straight bar.

A snaffle with two joints acts on the bars of the mouth and the lips. It has no nutcracker action. It may drop down on the tongue.

☐ A thick mouthpiece is milder than a thin one.
☐ Eggbutt rings are less likely to pinch the lips or corners of the mouth than are loose, flat ring or cheek snaffles.
☐ A loose ring snaffle allows more movement in the mouthpiece and encourages a horse to champ the bit.
☐ The severity of the bit is increased by any uneven or squared-off bearing surface: i.e. twisted, plated, roller.
☐ A straight bar snaffle puts pressure on the tongue and then the bars.
☐ A cheek or Fulmer snaffle correctly fitted can give more control over a strong or uneducated horse unwilling to accept brakes or direction. The cheeks do not pull through the mouth, and when a direct rein is used, pressure is brought to bear on the other side of the horse's face and on the bars of the mouth. All cheeked snaffles help to keep a horse straight.

☐ A cheek snaffle used without keepers puts more pressure on the corners of the mouth, lips and tongue and less on the bars.

TYPES OF SNAFFLE

Single Joint
FLAT RING. There is some risk of pinching the lips.
EGGBUTT. This prevents rubbing at the corners of the lips.
GERMAN LOOSE RING HOLLOW MOUTH. The mouthpiece has a broad, thick design. The hollow mouthpiece makes it light in weight.
D-RING RACE SNAFFLE. This is less likely to be pulled through the mouth.
LARGE RING RACING. This will not pull through the mouth.
FULMER or AUSTRALIAN. Keepers are attached from the top of the cheek to the bridle, which keep the bit upright and still in the mouth. They also prevent the joint from dropping down on the tongue. This bit is made of solid metal and can be heavy.
CHEEK. This should have keepers so that the joint is kept off the tongue. It can be a useful bit on a young horse. All cheek snaffles help to keep a horse straight.

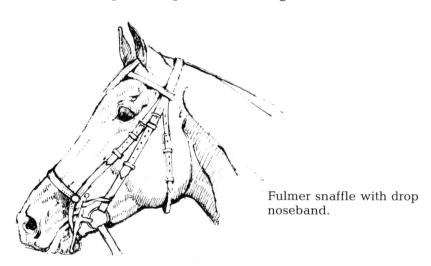

Fulmer snaffle with drop noseband.

SPOON. This can have full cheeks or half cheeks, which can be either above or below the mouthpiece. The latter type is used for driving.

HANGING CHEEK. This suspends the bit in the mouth and gives more room for the tongue. It can be useful for horses who put their tongue over the bit.

TWISTED. This is severe because of the ridged surface.

Double Joint

FRENCH BRIDOON. This has a rounded plate which joins the two parts of the snaffle. The plate lies flat on the tongue. There is no nutcracker action from this bit, and many horses – particularly if a little set in the jaw – relax and go better. If this bit has square arms, or a sharp-edged plate, it is not allowed in dressage tests.

DICK CHRISTIAN. This has a small ring joining the two arms which removes the nutcracker action and gives room for the tongue. Some horses resent the pressure of the small ring.

DR BRISTOL. This has a plate with squared edges fixed between the two arms. The bit is severe, but when the flat plate is on the tongue it is less sharp than when the bit is turned the other way, and the plate goes across the tongue. It should never be used reversed.

Straight Bar

VULCANITE LOOSE RING.

NYLON. This has a half-moon or mullen mouthpiece.

RUBBER. This is a very mild bit, but not durable.

METAL LOOSE RING.

The above bits are more comfortable for the horse, and have a milder action if they are of half-moon or mullen design.

LEATHER BIT. There are several types of this bit on the market. One is made from strips of leather stitched over a lining of steel or copper wire. It has a soft, broad bearing surface, and is a kind bit, useful for a horse with a very sensitive mouth or with mouth problems, i.e. bruised tongue, sore bars.

Severe Snaffles

The bits below have a severe action, and none is permitted in dressage tests. Before resorting to such bits, expert advice should be sought. These bits should only be used when other methods of control have failed.

WILSON. This has four rings, the two attached to the mouthpiece take the reins, the other two take the headpiece. A severe squeezing on the face results when the reins are pulled.

MAGENIS. This has set in squared-off arms.

CHERRY ROLLER. This prevents the horse from catching hold of the bit and running away. The uneven surface is sharp to the tongue and bars.

'Y' or 'W'. The two mouthpieces can give a pinching action to the lips and tongue.

SCORRIER. This has a twisted mouthpiece, and two rings which act as 'Wilson Rings' (see above).

CORNISH or WATERFORD. This is composed of several thick jointed plates which are similar in shape to those of a French bridoon.

ROCKWELL, NORTON, NEWMARKET. These are forms of snaffle bridle which by various means produce pressure on the nose as well as on the mouth. They can be of some use on strong horses with uneducated mouths who have not been taught to obey, or who fight against more legitimate methods of control.

SPRING MOUTH. This attachment is clipped to the rings of a snaffle giving a double bit action.

CHAIN SNAFFLE. The mouthpiece is made of chain links.

TWISTED WIRE. This has two mouthpieces of twisted wire.

THE GAG SNAFFLE. A gag snaffle has two holes in the bit rings or cheeks, through which run roundings attached to the headpiece and ending in the reins. The mouthpiece is jointed and can be smooth, twisted or with rollers. It is generally used on its own, but can be operated as the bridoon part of a double bridle if greater control is required. Its action brings considerable pressure on the corners of the mouth and the poll. It can be effective on horses who put their heads down and pull, as its leverage action makes it possible for the rider to raise the horse's head. It should always have a second rein attached to the rings of the bit, which allows it to be used as a normal snaffle when the gag action is not required. This bridle used in the wrong hands can prove dangerous, making some horses rear. It should never be used by children or inexperienced adults.

The use of such bits indicates failure in the correct training of the horse. Frequently the bits create more confusion in the horse's mind, thus compounding the problem.

Snaffles for Use on Young Horses
KEY RING MOUTHING BIT. This is still used by some trainers. The keys encourage the horse to play with the bit, but may also encourage him to put his tongue over the bit. Modern training methods require that the horse should learn to hold the bit quietly in his mouth with a relaxed jaw. For this purpose, a jointed or mullen mouth snaffle is now more acceptable.
TATTERSALL YEARLING BIT. This is a circular bit sometimes used on yearlings to give greater control when being shown. The bit is attached to a show headcollar by short straps, and encircles the lower jaw with the key section in the mouth. The lead rein is attached to the back ring, and when used the bit rises up in the mouth.

Special Bits
CHIFNEY ANTI-REARING. This acts in a similar way to the normal ring bit, but if the horse should attempt to rear, the 'U' shape puts greater pressure on his tongue: therefore discouraging the habit. It is made of thin metal and is severe.
HORSESHOE CHEEK STALLION BIT. This is a showing bit and is buckled to a show headcollar. It has horseshoe-shaped cheeks, and a straight bar or mullen mouth bit which acts on the corners of the mouth, the tongue, and then the bars.

FITTING

To Fit a Snaffle Bit

The bit should fit the mouth. It should be neither too small, when it will pinch, or too large, when it will pull through the mouth. It should not protrude more than 0.5cm or ¼in on each side. A straight bar snaffle should not wrinkle the corners of the lips; a jointed snaffle should do so slightly.

THE DOUBLE BRIDLE

This has two metal bits. The bridoon is a snaffle bit with small rings. The curb has no joint, and comes in a variety of designs, but it must have a curb chain. Some types do not have 'Ds' for the lip strap.

The double bridle is used:
- ☐ On horses which having been trained in a snaffle are ready to understand and accept a lighter and more refined aid for the rider's hand.

- ☐ In the showing ring, where its purpose is not only to add to the horse's turnout but also to increase control.

- ☐ In the hunting field and competitive jumping. Its

Curb bit with curb chain and lip strap.

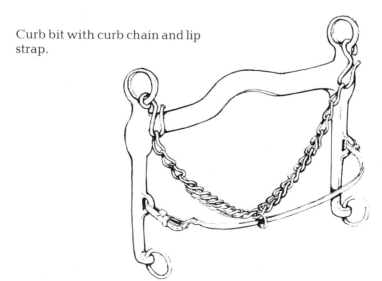

function is to help keep the horse in better balance, and to act as a more effective brake than the snaffle bridle. The latter, if on a strong horse, often results in the rider having to use considerable force and strength to retain control.

Action of double bridle bits on horses trained in a snaffle:
☐ The bridoon acts in a similar way to the snaffle. It asks the horse to work on the bit, going forward with an even contact on both hands.

☐ The curb bit, more correctly called 'the bit', gives a lighter and more refined aid. It helps to obtain collection from the horse. It also helps balance and control. It should lie immediately below the bridoon, but not so low that it touches the tushes. Both bits must be able to act independently.

The mouthpiece of the bit acts on the tongue and the bars of the mouth, and as a fulcrum for the upper and lower cheeks of the bit. When the curb rein is used, the curb chain tightens and applies pressure in the chin groove. As this occurs, the upper cheekpiece moves forward (its position governed by the tightness of the curb chain), and brings slight pressure to bear on the poll. The longer the lower cheek, the greater the pressure and severity of the action, both on the chin groove and the poll. A shallow tongue groove or port gives added room for the tongue; a high port presses on the roof of the mouth and can cause acute pain and distress.

The curb chain should be adjusted to ensure that the chain comes into action when the cheeks of the bit are at an angle of 45 degrees. If adjusted more loosely, both the bit and curb chain lose their true action and effectiveness. An adjustment tighter than 45 degrees gives a more effective action, and requires a more precise use of the curb rein.

Types of Bridoon
These can be loose ring or eggbutt. They can have

hanging cheeks and either one or two joints. The usual variations are:

☐ Ordinary bridoon with loose rings.
☐ Double-jointed bridoon with eggbutt rings.
☐ Hanging cheeked bridoon with one joint.

Types of Bit
These may have a tongue groove or port of variable height. The cheeks may also vary in length.
FIXED CHEEK with a low port and medium-length cheeks. This has a more immediate and precise action than the sliding mouthpiece.
WEYMOUTH SLIDING MOUTHPIECE with a low port and longer length cheeks. The mouthpiece moves up and down. The cheeks go through the mouthpiece, so that increased contact on one will bring the other into action.
THICK MOUTH GERMAN. This has a thick, fixed mouthpiece which tapers in the centre to allow room for the tongue. The mouthpiece can be hollow. The cheeks can be straight or curve forward. Many thoroughbred horses are uncomfortable in this bit owing to its thickness.
HALF-MOON OR MULLEN MOUTH. This has short, fixed cheeks and a half-moon mouthpiece which allows some room for the tongue: though when the curb rein is used, pressure falls more on the tongue than on the bars.
BANBURY. The mouthpiece is a round bar which is slotted through the cheeks. It has no port. It can revolve to give an independent action to each cheek, and to the corresponding curb rein. It may also be made to move up and down. It is now rarely used.

CURB CHAINS

These can be of metal, with either single or double links. They can also be of leather or elastic. Rubber or leather curb guards can be fixed to metal chains. For fitting see page 30.

Pelham bit with double-link curb chain through bit ring.

THE PELHAM

This bit is a combination of a snaffle and a double bridle. It has one bit, the mouthpiece of which can be jointed, straight or half-moon (mullen), either with or without a port. It has a lower cheek, which takes the curb chain. It usually has two reins: one attached to the rings on the mouthpiece and the other to the rings on the lower cheek. It may be fitted with roundings on the bit and one rein. Some Pelhams do not have a lip strap. The longer the cheek, the greater the leverage.

The Pelham can be said to have a rather indefinite action, but many horses and particularly ponies appear to work happily in it. It cannot be considered as a bit likely to improve a horse's mouth, but its use by an uneducated or heavy handed rider probably does less harm to the horse's mouth. With a long-jawed horse it can be difficult to get the curb chain pressure in the chin groove.

Types of Pelham:
MULLEN MOUTH. This is widely used. The mouthpiece can be made of metal, vulcanite, nylon or rubber.
JOINTED. This can be smooth or twisted, and has a more severe action than the mullen or vulcanite.
VULCANITE. A mild type of Pelham, which seems to suit

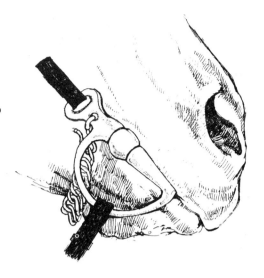

Kimblewick bit with curb chain.

a variety of horses whose owners find them too strong in a snaffle.

KIMBLEWICK. A single-rein Pelham with a port and rounded ends. The mouthpiece can be of metal or vulcanite. It is a strong bit, which some sensitive horses resent. It can be used on ponies who are too strong for their child riders in a snaffle. As with all strong bits, its continual use soon deadens a horse's mouth.

SHOW HACK and GLOBE CHEEK. These are curb bits used without the bridoon, and only have one rein attached. They are seen on show ponies and occasionally show hacks. They are severe, and need to be used with a light hand.

RUBBER. This is a soft version of the vulcanite. It can encourage horses to chew and then tends to get worn through.

ARMY REVERSIBLE or UNIVERSAL. This was designed for army use to suit as many different types of horses as possible. It is reversible, allowing either the smooth or the twisted side of the bit to be in action. The top rein is attached to 'D'-shaped rings; the lower rein can be used in either of two slots according to need. It does not have a lip strap.

THREE-IN-ONE or SWALES. This is a very severe bit. It

acts without poll pressure, the headpiece being supported by rings on the mouthpiece. When the curb rein is used, very severe pressure is put on the chin groove. If the top rein only is used, it is much less severe and many horses go well in it.

THE BITLESS BRIDLE OR HACKAMORE

This bridle is designed to control the horse by applying pressure on the nose without the use of a bit. It can be effective on horses with damaged mouths, or on those who through bad handling resent and fight a normal bridle. It gives good control, but steering can be difficult.

It consists of a bridle head, cheeks, and padded noseband held in place by a strap or chain. Reins are attached to rings on the noseband, and these apply pressure via the strap or chain. Considerable leverage is obtained on the nose, and to a lesser degree on the poll, the chin groove and the lower jaw. The precise action depends on the design of the bridle. Some hackamores can be very severe and should only be used by riders aware of their action and capable of using them with tact and discretion. They should not be used on ponies or by uneducated riders.

A simpler form of control — but which is only suitable for exercising in a confined space — consists of two rings attached to a well-padded and firmly fixed dropped noseband.

BIT ATTACHMENTS

RUBBER BIT GUARDS fit on each side of the bit, and protect the face and corners of the lips of a sensitive horse.
TONGUE GRIDS are made of metal, and are held in place by a separate head strap. They are fitted into the horse's mouth above the normal bit to prevent a horse putting his tongue over the bit.
RUBBER TONGUE GRIDS fit on to a narrow straight bar

snaffle and may help to prevent a horse putting his tongue over the bit. It is important to check that they cannot be easily dislodged, as they may either be spat out by the horse or swallowed.

AUSTRALIAN CHEEKER. This is a rubber device running from the headpiece down the front of the horse's face. Attached to each side of the bit, it helps to keep the bit high in the mouth, and prevents a horse getting his tongue over the bit. It is most often used on racehorses.

CHAPTER 5
Boots and Bandages

BOOTS

Boots are used to protect a horse's legs and joints from injury, either self-inflicted or from an outside source. Self-inflicted injuries are the result of:

☐ Faulty conformation.
☐ Faulty action.
☐ Poor shoeing.
☐ Lack of balance in a young horse.
☐ Poor condition and lack of muscle.
☐ Fatigue.
☐ Careless riding.
☐ Galloping in deep going.
☐ Pecking over a fence.

Types of Injury
BRUSHING. This occurs on the inside of the leg below the knee or hock. It is inflicted by the opposite foot, usually in the area of the fetlock joint.

SPEEDICUT. This occurs when a horse is galloping and cuts into the leg just below the knee or hock with the opposite front or hind foot.

LOW OVER-REACH. This is a bruise or cut on the heel of a front foot. The front foot stays on the ground too long, and the inside edge of the hind shoe strikes down into the heel. It usually occurs over a jump, when an extra effort has been made and the jump was unbalanced, or the landing in deep going. However, big-moving horses can lose their balance on the flat and over-reach.

HIGH OVER-REACH. This is an injury to the back tendon caused by the horse when over-jumping or losing balance when galloping. The front of the hind foot or front outside toe edges strikes into the back of the front leg below the knee. It is always serious, even if there is no cut. When caused by another horse it is referred to as 'struck into'. All over-reaches must be treated seriously as they entail internal bruising and a possible seat of infection.

TREAD. This can be self-inflicted, when a horse treads on the inner coronet of one front foot with the other front foot. It can occur during travelling or with a weaver.

Injury from another horse treading on the outside of the coronet can occur:

- When travelling with another horse if there is no partition.
- During a game of polo.
- Among a restless group of horses: i.e. out hunting.
- When riding one horse and leading another.
- Riding too close behind another horse.

Treads can be serious if they cause internal bruising.

BRUISED SHINS. These are caused by rapping either front or hind shins on a jump.

POLO KNOCKS. These can occur anywhere on the legs; but they happen more usually on the front legs below the knee. They are caused by a blow from a polo stick or from the ball.

Use of Boots

When schooling valuable horses of any age it is a sensible precaution to fit protective boots according to the work to be done. This often saves an unnecessary injury, which could lay the horse off work.

Boots are not advisable when out hunting or on long distance rides, as mud works up under the boot. Pressures and friction over several hours will cause a sore place, which can quickly become infected and cause acute lameness.

Boots are designed to give protection to a specified area of the horse's leg. In some cases, it may be necessary to have them individually made to alleviate a particular problem.

Materials
Boots are made of synthetic material, leather (usually lined with sheepskin or foam rubber) or heavy cloth such as Kersey or box cloth (a lighter material) • Regardless of material, it is important that after use, boots are either brushed clean, or if wet, washed • Leather boots and fastenings must be kept supple • Leather or cloth boots, if not well cleaned, become hard and cause pressure sores on a horse's leg. These can quickly become infected, resulting in a lame horse • Synthetic material is less likely to cause this problem, but cleaning after use is still essential. Synthetics are lighter, more comfortable for the horse, and easier to clean or wash. They are generally preferable to boots made of traditional materials.

Fastenings
Boots should always fasten on the outside of the leg, with the end of the strap pointing towards the rear. Fastenings can be buckles, clips or Velcro. Front leg boots should have three or four fastenings. Hind leg boots, which are longer, should have four or five. A short type of boot may have only one fastening.

Leather boots always have sewn-on leather straps and buckles. These are secure, but are time-consuming to fasten, and the stitching needs regular inspection.

Kersey, box cloth and synthetic material have buckles, clips or self-holding Velcro fastenings.

Fastenings are often set on strong elastic, which makes the boots more comfortable for the horse. The elastic must be regularly inspected. If it becomes stretched and loses its strength it must be renewed.

Boots and Bandages

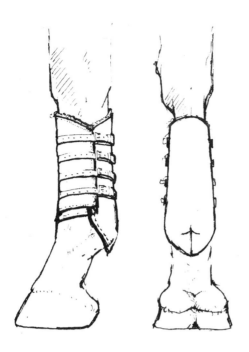

Brushing boots.

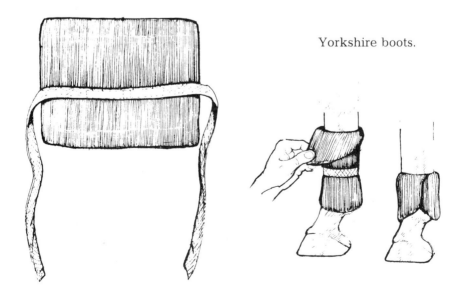

Yorkshire boots.

If Velcro is used, make sure that the straps are wide enough and long enough, so that the boot is held securely. The Velcro must always be kept clean. If it wears smooth it must be renewed. As Velcro fastenings are easily dislodged in rough conditions, they are not suitable for hacking through mud or for cross-country work.

Types of Protective Boot

BRUSHING BOOT. This is full size and protects the whole of the inside of the leg below the knee, including the fetlock joint. The boot should be placed on the leg rather higher than in its final position. It should be firmly fastened, starting from the top, and then eased a little down the leg so that it protects the fetlock joint. The boots should then be checked to see that they are firm, cannot move about, but are not too tight.

FETLOCK BOOT. This is a short boot, usually of leather, with one strap. It gives protection to the fetlock joint only.

YORKSHIRE BOOT. This is usually put on a hind joint. It is a piece of heavy cloth about 30cms (12ins) long and 20cms (8ins) broad, with wide tape or Velcro stitched about two-thirds down its length. It is then wound round the leg, fastened on the outside above the fetlock joint and eased down over the joint. The cloth above the tape is then folded over to form a double thickness. Note that in deep going the boot can be sucked off.

RUBBER RING. This is a hollow ring with a leather or metal fastening running through its centre. It can be used round the horse's pastern or above the fetlock joint, and protects either area.

SAUSAGE BOOT. This is a large, leather-covered, padded ring. It is fastened round the pastern, and prevents a horse bruising an elbow with the heel of the same front foot when lying down.

SPEEDICUTTING BOOT. This is similar to a full-length brushing boot, but is cut to come higher up the leg and to give greater protection to the inner lower part of the knee or hock.

OVER-REACH BOOT. This is a bell-shaped boot made of rubber. It is pulled on over the foot: which can be difficult, but if the boot is turned inside out and soaked in hot water, the rubber becomes more pliable and the task easier. It can also be fastened round the pastern: which though it is easier to put on, the boot can move round and the fastening itself cause an injury.

TENDON BOOT. This is shaped like a brushing boot, but has extra padding down the back of the leg to protect the tendon from being struck into.

CORONET BOOT. This is a small, semi-circular covering, usually of leather. It fastens round the pastern, and protects the coronet. It is used for polo or travelling. Horses can easily tread on themselves or one another if travelling without

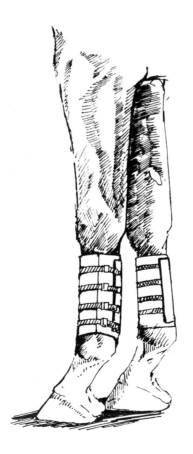

Tendon boots.

a partition. The bruising may be invisible, but can be quite severe. Bandages and Gamgee give some protection if they are put on to reach down over the coronet, but coronet boots can be a wise precaution.

POLO BOOT. This is similar to a brushing boot, but is made of heavy felt, and is longer – coming well down the fetlock. Some types which cover the coronet also strap round the pastern. The boots are put on in the usual way, or they may be secured with firm bandages, the latter being fastened with cotton or self-adhesive tape and the ends sewn for extra security.

HEEL BOOT. Racehorses and eventers, when galloping, sometimes injure the point of the fetlock joint around the ergot. A brushing boot, cut lower at the back and shaped to the joint, will prevent this.

EQUIBOOT. This is a patented boot made in varying sizes to fit over a horse's foot. It is used:

☐ To protect the foot if for any reason the horse cannot be shod and is required for work

☐ In the stable, to keep a foot poultice in place, especially for a horse which chews at bandages and sacking.

Its exact fit is very important. A boot which is too tight can bruise the heels and set up an infection. If it is too loose it will come off. The fit can be adjusted by tightening or loosening the heel pads at the back of the boot.

POULTICE BOOT. This is made of synthetic material or leather. Its purpose is to hold foot dressings in place. It fits over the foot and is fastened up the leg.

TREATMENT BOOT. This is similar to a wellington boot, and reaches from the foot to well above the knee. It is used for applying cold water treatment to an injured leg.

TRAVELLING BOOT. Many people use a well-applied stable bandage with a generous lining of Gamgee or similar material. Bandaging, however, takes time, and labour-saving alternatives are *leg guards* or *travelling boots*. These are made from synthetic materials, and have a thick, fleecy-type lining. They are fastened with several wide Velcro straps. They should be long enough to reach from above the knee and hock down over the coronet. It is then not necessary to use knee caps and hock boots. Young or nervous horses can be alarmed by the noise when the Velcro is pulled apart, and accidents have been known to be caused by their use.

Knee Caps

These are used for travelling or exercising on roads, and are made of leather, heavy cloth or synthetic material. To be smart, the material should match the rest of the travelling equipment ● The front of the knee cap is covered with a reinforced pad of leather ● The straps are leather ● The top strap should be set in strong elastic to allow it to be firmly fixed without causing the horse discomfort. It should be fastened well above the knee on the outside. The spare end of strap should be forwards. The knee cap can then be eased down and tested to make sure it cannot slip over the knee ● The bottom strap must be fastened very loosely, usually in the first hole, so that it cannot interfere with the action of the joint.

SKELETON KNEE CAPS. These are lightweight knee boots consisting of a top strap and a reinforced leather pad to cover the knee. When hacking out on roads, skeleton knee caps can be a wise protection. For general use they should

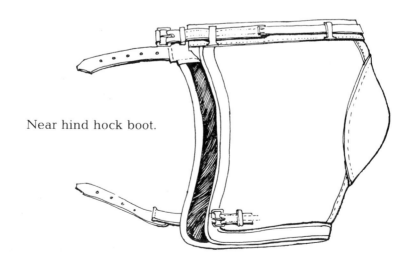

Near hind hock boot.

have two straps. For jumping, to prevent further bruising or to protect an old injury, they should have top straps only.

Hock Boots or Caps

Hock boots are designed to protect the point of the hock when travelling. They are of similar construction to knee caps. The top holding strap is usually set in strong elastic so that it can be firmly buckled without cramping the joint. It is fastened on the outside, quite close to the front of the hock. The bottom strap should be fastened more firmly than that of the knee cap but not too tightly. The spare end of strap should be towards the rear.

BANDAGES

Bandaging the Legs

Whichever type of bandage is used, it is essential for them to be correctly and skilfully applied. Badly or carelessly applied bandages can cause untold damage to a horse's legs.

Various methods of bandaging are acceptable, but the essential requirements are:
☐ The bandage must be correctly and firmly rolled. First, roll the tapes or fastenings in the position where they are stitched. Then roll the bandage round them.
☐ The bandage should be applied only as firmly as is needed to keep it in place and to prevent it slipping.
☐ It should be applied without wrinkles. The pressure should be minimal but even. The tapes should not be tied any tighter than the bandage.
☐ Tapes should be tied on the outside and the loose ends should be tucked away.

Causes of damage:
☐ Tapes and/or a bandage which is too tight, or a twisted bandage, can cause marks on the leg and possible tendon damage.
☐ Tapes tied at the back over the tendon may cause

severe injury. Tapes tied at the front are likely to bruise the cannon bone. Tied on the inside they are less secure than on the outside.

☐ A poorly applied bandage can slip down and become dislodged when the horse stands up after resting. It may then be stepped on and torn.

Types of Bandage

STABLE BANDAGES are used:

☐ For warmth and to keep the circulation active.
☐ To assist in the drying-off of wet legs.
☐ For keeping poultices in position. Crepe bandage can also be used for this.
☐ To protect the legs whilst travelling.
☐ As a support for a sound leg when the opposite one is being treated for injury.

EXERCISE BANDAGES are used as a protection against injury during work.

SURGICAL BANDAGES are used to cover and protect wounds, for poulticing of the leg when there is a likelihood of swelling, and for wounds on joints. They are usually made of a synthetic stretch material.

TAIL BANDAGES are used:

☐ In the stable to help keep a tail tidy.
☐ When travelling, as a protection, both for the tail hair and the dock.

Leg Wraps

These give added protection and warmth.

GAMGEE is cotton wool in a muslin cover. It gives the best protection, but is expensive and is easily soiled. If the edges of the Gamgee are machine stitched, it is easier to wash and will last longer.

LEG WRAPS are thick felt pads cut to fit the leg. They are more expensive, but are quick to put on, easy to wash, and durable. In the long term they are very economical.

FIBREGEE is a man-made cloth, similar to thick felt. It is easily washed and durable.

FOAM RUBBER is cheap and easy to wash, but can draw the leg, and some horses are allergic to it.

HAY OR STRAW can be used for drying off wet legs. Pummel it well, then wrap it round the leg before bandaging. This is known as 'thatching'.

Bandage Fastenings

TAPE. This should be wide and flat. When the bandage is washed, the tape should be smoothed out and, if necessary, ironed flat.

VELCRO. This is a rough synthetic material, and is self-holding. It is efficient and easy to use as long as it is kept clean. In a shavings bed it can become impregnated with dirt, and then will not hold securely. It must also be long enough to secure the bandage.

CLIPS. These are satisfactory for stable bandages, but their shape can cause unnecessary pressure.

SELF-ADHESIVE TAPES. These are separate from the bandage. They are an expensive means of fastening bandages, but are secure. For extra security during competition, racing, or strenuous work, the end of the tapes should be sewn to the bandage. Surgical and crepe bandages are usually fastened with adhesive tape.

1. Stable Bandages

These can be made of wool, stockinette or man-made fibre. thermal bandages are also available; one type keeps the leg warm, and the other cold; the latter can be useful after an injury. Full-size bandages should be 10 to 12cms (4 to 5ins) wide x 2.1 to 2.4m (7 to 8ft) long. Unless of double thickness – i.e. Newmarket bandages – they should be always used with padding underneath.

Additional requirements:

Poulticing the leg. A double thickness of Gamgee is often used for extra protection should there be a tendency for the leg to swell.

Travelling. The Gamgee or other lining should extend well up over the knee and well down over the coronet. The bandage is applied as already described.

Boots and Bandages

Support Bandages. A horse who injures a front leg is likely to put more weight on the other leg, which can result in a strain. A supporting bandage firmly applied over a thick layer of Gamgee will help to avert this.

To Put on Stable Bandages

- Place the lining around the leg. It should show 1.2cms (½in) above and below the finished bandage.
- Start bandaging in the same direction as the overlap of the lining, just below the knee or hock.
- If the bandage is too short, start just above the joint, apply down to the coronet, and then back up the leg to the knee or hock.
- Many people prefer the latter method of bandaging as it is more likely to discourage filled legs: the bandage being put on upwards towards the heart.
- Place 10cms (4ins) of the bandage at an angle above the first round, which should be pulled firm, and should hold the flap of the bandage in place. This flap can now be folded down, so that the rest of the rounds of bandage help to secure it.

Putting on a support bandage.

- Roll the bandage down the leg. About half the width of the bandage should be left exposed on each circuit. It should not be necessary to alter the angle or to pull the bandage.
- When nearing the coronet, unroll the bandage in a similar upwards direction, finishing just below the knee or hock.
- The tapes or fastenings should finish on the outside of the leg. The tapes should be tied in a neat bow with the ends tucked in.

The legs of a stabled horse can fill due to:
☐ Strenuous exercise.
☐ Standing in for a day.
☐ An old injury.
☐ A stomach upset.
☐ Old age.
Such 'legs' usually walk down, but well-applied stable bandages at night help to keep the legs warm and the circulation active, which alleviates the problem.

2. Exercise Bandages

These should be made of stretch material: stockinette, elastic, crepe or elastic material. They should be 8cms (3ins) wide and 1.8 to 2.1m (6 to 7ft) long.

To Put on Exercise Bandages
It is usual to put Gamgee or other lining under the bandage to give added protection, and to ensure that the bandage and tapes do not mark or injure the leg.

The requirements and likely faults are similar to those of stable bandages, except that, being more elastic, and being used for work, these bandages require to be put on much more firmly.

The flap over at the top should be longer. When folded down under the rest of the bandage, this helps to keep it firm.

The bandage should extend from below the knee to the

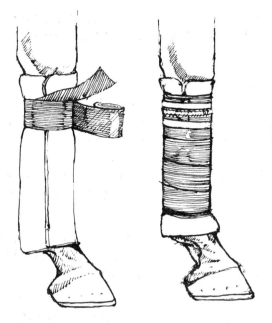

Putting on an exercise bandage.

fetlock joint. Stockinette or crepe bandages should not extend over the joint, as this may cause interference. Vetrap bandages, expertly applied, can be fitted over the joint for extra support and protection. They should be sewn or taped for extra security when going across country. Elastic bandages when worn for any length of time will contract if they get wet and then dry. This can cause serious discomfort and possible injury to the horse, by restricting circulation. It is therefore essential to use Gamgee or similar lining.

The Purpose of Exercise Bandages
Exercise bandages are often used to ease the strain on tendons and ligaments in the front leg, but are unlikely to do so. Their main purpose is to protect the leg from bruising when hitting a jump, and to avoid cutting and bruising the back of the front tendon by an over-reach or blow on the inner surface of the opposite front leg. If the bandages are used in muddy conditions for several hours, the mud is likely to work up underneath the bandage, leading to friction and possibly infection.

Various new types of reinforced lining are now produced

which can be cut to fit the leg. Used under an exercise bandage they give good protection from tendon injury for competition horses.

Removing Leg Bandages
Undo the fastening and, using both hands, unwind the bandage and remove the lining • Shake the linings and bandages out • If they are dirty, wash them. If they are damp, hang them up to dry • When the bandages are dry, roll up the tapes. Position them where they are sewn. Roll the bandages as firmly as possible over them, and tuck in the ends.

Bandages should be put away in twos or fours. Unroll enough of one bandage to wrap it around one or three other bandages, and secure by tucking in the flap.

Never use dirty bandages. Soiled material is stiff and hard, and is not suitable for either legs or tail • Elastic bandages should be frequently washed to retain their elasticity. Their correct application is then made easier.

When the bandages have been removed and before they are rolled, the horse's legs should be given a brisk rub in an upwards direction to stimulate circulation.

3. Tail Bandages
These are made of stockinette, crepe or elastic. They should be 6 to 8cms (2½ to 3ins) wide, and about 1.5 to 1.8m (5 to 6ft) long.
   Correctly applied they will improve the appearance of the tail. They should only be left on for a few hours in the day after grooming, and should be removed at night. Left on too long they can cause discomfort and restrict circulation, leading to a sore under the tail and ultimately to death of the bone and loss of the tail. When applying the bandage it is important to ensure that it is firm but not pulled too tight, and that the tapes are not tied tighter than the bandage itself.

To Put on a Tail Bandage
- Hold the bandage in one hand and lift up the tail. Put it over the shoulder or hold it up with the other hand.
- Place the spare end of the bandage under the tail and out at an angle at the top of the tail.
- Hold this spare end, and put one or two rounds of bandage as high up as possible round the tail.
- Turn down the flap and roll the bandage firmly down the tail to just below the dock.
- Tie it firmly, but not too tight.
- To give extra security, when bandaging an unpulled tail, take a small wisp of hair and put it over the first twist of the bandage and under the second.

To Remove a Tail Bandage
- Undo the tapes, and with both hands pull the bandage down from the top. It should come away complete • Shake it out and roll it up • Dirty bandages should always be washed before they are put away • If a tail has been plaited, the bandage must be unwound, not pulled off.

CHAPTER 6
Clothing

RUGS

Clothing includes the various rugs, blankets and sheets worn by the stabled horse. He requires rugs in winter to keep him warm, in summer to protect him from flies and to keep his coat clean. All stable and day rugs are secured by a front fastening. A leather roller or webbing surcingle can then be fixed round the body. The roller may or may not have a breast girth. Modern rugs have cross-over surcingles and fastenings under the belly, or just leg straps.

Types of Rug
Stable or Night Rug
This can be made of hemp, jute, canvas or synthetic material. HEMP RUGS are lightweight and are usually only half-lined with blanket. They are suitable for ponies and small horses, but will not stand up to as much hard usage as jute or canvas rugs. The fully lined, heavy-duty JUTE or CANVAS RUG – although more expensive – lasts longer, stands regular washing and is recommended for the larger type of horse. SYNTHETIC RUGS made of polyester and other man-made fibres are more expensive but are light, warm, comfortable, easily washed, and more easily kept in place. They usually have a polyester filling. They offer improved temperature control and better air flow to provide insulation.

Clothing

Blankets

These are worn under the stable rug for extra warmth. They are usually made from THICK WOOLLEN CLOTH. BLANKETS are sold in different sizes, by weight. They are expensive but last many years and repay the outlay. LIGHTWEIGHT BLANKETS are a cheap alternative, but are not as warm, and they tear more easily. MAN-MADE FIBRE BLANKETS can be shaped like a rug and they fasten across the chest.

Aerborn or Sweat Rug

There are many different types available. The large cotton mesh type is used to help cool off a horse. It works on the principle of a string vest – forming air pockets – and effectively insulates the horse against chill. For it to work efficiently, it is essential to put a top rug or sheet over it. Worn on its own, it helps to keep flies away, but it has little other value. Sweat rugs made of cotton towelling do not need a top rug to work efficiently.

Day Rug

This rug is worn for a special occasion, such as for competition work. It is made of wool, and is available in a variety of colours. It is buckled in front. The hems are braided, and it usually has the initials of the school or owner on the bottom corner.

Summer Sheet

This comes in a variety of colours or checks, and is made of cotton, linen or synthetic material. In hot weather it protects the horse against flies and keeps the coat tidy and clean. In warm weather it is used instead of a day rug for horses travelling to competitions and for special occasions. It can be put over a sweat sheet in summer.

As it is light in weight, it is kept in place by a fillet string, which lies round the quarters and under the tail. The string is attached to both edges of the sheet about halfway down.

Exercise Sheet or Paddock Sheet

This is usually made of lightweight wool, and matches

the day rug in colour. It can be used under the saddle for exercise in dry cold winter weather. For racing, it is worn in the paddock over the saddle. It reaches from the horse's withers and shoulder to the top of the dock, and is kept in place by a lightweight, matching roller or surcingle. Fillet strings are essential. When used under the saddle, the sheet should have tape loops through which the girth runs, to prevent it from slipping back.

Waterproof Rug
This is made from waterproof fabric, and can be lined or unlined. A lining helps to absorb any sweat and allows the skin to breathe. The waterproof rug is used at competitions, or on occasions when hacking in very cold, wet weather. A fillet string is essential.

Hoods and Caps
Racehorses are often exercised in cold weather wearing a hood, or a cap which is a shortened version of the hood. They are made of lightweight, coloured cloth, and are of value to well-bred horses on walking exercise in very cold weather. It can be of waterproof fabric, and used in conjunction with a waterproof rug.

New Zealand Rug
This is worn:
☐ By horses and ponies living out in the winter, to protect them from wind and rain. It also helps to keep the horses clean.
☐ To protect stabled horses and ponies who are turned out during the day. The rug keeps them warm and comparatively clean.
The rugs are made of lined waterproof canvas or man-made fibre. Investigation into materials continues, and improved types are constantly coming on the market. The canvas type is heavier and stands up to harder use, but the lighter nylon rug is less likely to rub, and is easier to keep in place. Canvas rugs in the original design have no roller and are self-righting when the horse rolls. Other makes have

a stitched surcingle, which is eased over the backbone to avoid pressure. Both ends pass through the side of the rug. Nylon rugs are either buckled under the girth, or with cross-over surcingles or have leg straps. There is now a lightweight material on the market which is waterproof and allows the skin to breathe. The extra expense is justified by the well being of the animal.

It is essential for a New Zealand rug to fit correctly. It should lie snugly round the neck, so that it cannot work back and rub the top of the withers. It should reach to the top of the tail. Sheepskin pads can be sewn to prevent chafing, though – especially with a fixed surcingle – the pads restrict the flow of air under the rug, resulting in condensation. Leg straps can either be passed round the upper thigh and clipped on to the rug on the same side, or crossed to the opposite site. They should fit neither tightly nor too loosely. They must allow room for the horse to move.

When animals are living out all the time in New Zealand rugs two rugs should be available so that a wet one can be dried.

New Zealand rugs can cause severe rubbing and – if neglected – open sores. Animals at grass should have their rugs checked twice a day. The leg straps, if of leather, should be kept clean and oiled. The nylon straps of fibre rugs seem to cause less friction. If canvas rugs become worn, they can be reproofed by painting with a waterproof paint such as that used on tents.

Always put a New Zealand rug on in the stable. Although it is not intended for wear in the stable, allow the horse to get used to it before turning him out. If the horse is likely to gallop when first turned out, it is safer to turn him out without a rug for twenty minutes and then catch him and put on the rug. Alternatively, he may be walked and trotted with the rug on before letting him loose. The following day, the horse should have settled and can be turned out wearing the rug initially.

ROLLERS

Rollers are used to keep rugs in place ● They are made of leather or webbing, and are placed round the horse just behind his withers ● Leather rollers are very expensive, but they last many years ● Good-quality webbing is less expensive, but it becomes worn comparatively quickly ● Cheap jute webbing is only suitable for ponies, and will not stand hard wear ● It is important to buy a width of webbing roller suitable to the size of the horse as rollers of narrow width quickly deteriorate if worn by a full-size horse ● Be sure to choose the correct length. Remember that if a fat horse loses weight or when extra blankets and wither pads are removed – the roller will become loose.

A PLAIN ROLLER has padding on either side of the spine. Even so, a thick foam rubber pad should always be put under the roller to minimise pressure on the spine and withers.

AN ANTI-CAST or ARCH ROLLER is used for horses who habitually roll over in their stable and get cast ● It can have a fixed or adjustable arch, and comes in a normal size, a small arch, or a giant-size arch ● The giant size is more likely to prevent the horse getting cast ● The small arch can be useless if the horse has a thick straw bed ● The main drawback to an arched roller is that although it removes all pressure from the spine, it concentrates it on either side of the withers. Even if a thick pad is used, it can have a severe pinching effect ● An arch roller should have buckles on both sides, so that if a horse gets cast, it is possible to release the roller and then right the horse.

Rollers used over a day rug, summer or paddock sheet are usually made of matching woollen or cotton web.

Breast Girth or Breast Strap

This is a strap made of leather or webbing. It has a buckle at each end, which is fastened to a leather strap threaded through the 'Ds' placed on either side of the roller ● The purpose of the breast girth is to prevent the roller from sliding back: which can easily happen with a fit or thin horse ● The breast girth should rest close to, but not tightly, around the chest and just above the point of the shoulder.

Surcingles

Webbing surcingles are stitched on to a night rug, and take the place of rollers ● They should not be stitched over the top of the back, as the surcingle should be loose in this area ● If two surcingles are used, one should be stitched about 46 to 60cms (18ins to 2ft) behind the other ● This provides a very secure arrangement for holding a rug in place ● The second surcingle need not be fastened tightly.

A most effective alternative is to use two surcingles stitched at an angle on the sides of the rug and crossed over under the belly. They are usually referred to as 'cross-over surcingles' and are fastened with a flat metal clasp. This type of surcingle removes all pressures from the spine and holds rugs in place efficiently.

Belly Straps

These are wide pieces of matching material used to hold in place a polyester or nylon quilted rug. They are attached to the bottom edge of the rug approximately 16cms (6ins) behind the elbow, and are fastened under the belly.

Leg Straps

Leg straps, as used for New Zealand rugs, can hold a lightweight man-made fibre rug in place. A roller should not be necessary. For fitting see 'New Zealand Rug' page 85.

MEASURING AND PUTTING ON RUGS

Measuring for a Rug

To find a correct size of rug, measure the horse from the centre of the breastbone along the side to the point of the quarters. Alternatively, measure from a point just in front of the withers to just above the top of the tail.

Putting on a Rug

A correctly fitted rug is comfortable for the horse, stays in place better, and lasts longer – as the material will be less subject to wear and tear. It should fit snugly, not loosely, round the neck. If it is too large in the neck, it may slip back, tighten over the withers, and eventually cause a sore. Also, when the horse gets up he can catch a foot in the neck, and in struggling he may hurt himself and tear the rug. If it is too tight, it will cause discomfort through pressure on the windpipe. It should cover the body down to the elbows and extend as far back as the dock. Sheepskin pads on the top inside part of the neck aid comfort, particularly for horses with high withers.

To Put on a Rug and Blanket

Use either a surcingle or roller with attached breast girth:

Method 1
- Tie up the horse.
- Collect up the blanket; the left side in the left hand and the right side in the right hand.
- Speak to the horse and then gently throw the blanket on to his neck and withers.
- Adjust the rug in front, so that it is even on both sides, and then bring the blanket back over the loins and quarters to just above the top of the tail.
- The front part of the blanket should lie well up the neck. If it does not, remove it and start again.
- A rug or blanket must never be pulled forward, as this ruffles the hairs of the coat and causes discomfort.
- Horse blankets usually have stripes either side. If these run lengthways they can be used to judge the correct position of the blanket on the back.
- It is essential always to put on the blanket the same way, so that any soiled area is at the quarters.
- The blanket can be turned back on itself. Approximately

16cms (6ins) should show in front of the stable rug. Alternatively, it can be turned back over the front of the stable rug. This helps to stop it slipping back at the withers.

- Finally, take hold of the stable rug, with your hands about 46 to 60cms (18 to 24ins) on either side of the centre seam. Gather it up and throw it gently over the neck and withers. Fasten the buckle, then draw the rug back over the quarters. As long as the horse is quiet, it helps to stand immediately behind him to make sure that both rugs are even and correctly placed.

If one or two attached surcingles are used, check on the off side that they are not twisted, and then buckle them firmly, but not too tightly, on the near side. The first surcingle *must be correctly placed on the rug*, and should fit where the girth would normally go. Cross-over surcingles must also be checked for twisting, and then fastened on the near side.

To Put on a Roller and Pad
A foam rubber pad about 46cms (18ins) long x 16cms (6ins) wide, 5cms (2ins) thick can be used ● Take the roller and pad and move to the off side of the horse ● Place the pad on top of the rug just behind the withers ● Put the short side of the roller over the back, and allow the long side to hang down ● Move to the near side, and if using a breast girth bring the end of it round and buckle to the roller ● Buckle up the main part of the roller firmly but not too tight. Run the hand down to smooth any blanket and rug wrinkles. The rug may now be eased a little forward at the bottom to free the elbows.

Method II
For this, a separate roller must always be used, preferably with a breast girth.

- Tie up the horse.
- Fold the blanket in half and place it well up over the neck and withers.

- Draw back the top half, making sure that it is straight and even, and ease it towards the tail.
- Fold up both front corners of the blanket so that they lie on top of the withers.
- Fold the stable rug and put it on as the blanket.
- Fold back the layer of blanket over the withers, so that it will go under the roller.
- Place the pad on top of the folded blanket and then fit the roller as before.

To Take Off a Rug and Blanket
- Tie up the horse.
- Unfasten the front buckle of the rug.
- Unfasten the surcingle or the roller and breast girth.
- Take it/them off and fold up.
- If the bedding is of straw, put them in a corner of the box, on the manger, or over the door.
- If the bed is of shavings, put them on the manger or over the door, not on the shavings.
- Next, fold both rugs back and then draw them off over the tail. Do not *pull* them off sideways, as this will ruffle the coat.
- Fold up the rugs and put with the roller.

When saddling up in cold weather, the rugs may be turned back sufficiently to allow the saddle to be put on, and then turned back over the saddle. If they have slipped back, do not pull them forward. Take them off and replace them separately. If the horse is left with his saddle on, he must be tied up.

The blanket or rug next to the skin should be taken out and brushed each day, but well away from the horse. It is helpful to have a second night rug, as this enables stained rugs to be washed.

CHAPTER 7
Care and Cleaning

CLEANING AND STORAGE OF CLOTHING

- ☐ Before clothing is put away in store, it must be washed or cleaned and, if necessary, sent for repair. If it is put away dirty, the ingrained manure rots the material, so the rope and blankets tear more easily and the rollers and surcingles break.
- ☐ Woollen day rugs and blankets should be well brushed, and then sent to be cleaned.
- ☐ Badly stained blankets may need laundering.
- ☐ Stable or night rugs can either be sent to a laundry, washed in a launderette or at home.
- ☐ Webbing rollers and surcingles should be washed at home, so that the leather fittings can be kept oiled. If they are soaked in hot water, they will become brittle and will break.
- ☐ Leather rollers should be washed clean and then treated with Kochaline, neatsfoot oil or dubbin.

Washing Rugs, Rollers and Surcingles at Home
- ☐ Before starting the washing, all leatherwork should be oiled. Alternatively, fittings can be removed and sewn on later.
- ☐ The rugs should be soaked in cold water in a dustbin or yard water trough. The water should be changed several times. The rugs can then be laid out on clean concrete and scrubbed with hot detergent or soap. A hose is a useful accessory.

☐ Rinse them in cold water in a yard water trough which is not used for horse's drinking water.
☐ Put more oil on the leatherwork and buckles.
☐ Hang them up to dry.
☐ With rollers and surcingles, it is necessary only to soak the dirty section and then wash it.
☐ Oil the leatherwork and buckles.
☐ Hang them up to dry.

Storage
☐ Rugs should be stored in rug boxes or on shelves.
☐ Moth preventatives should be put with them.
☐ Check them regularly for mice.
☐ Make sure that the room is dry and that the rugs are well aired and clean before putting them away.

CARE AND CLEANING OF LEATHER

For safety, appearance and durability, it is essential that all leather is kept clean and supple. Water, heat, sweat and neglect are its greatest enemies.

During use, leather loses a certain amount of oil and fat, which are drawn out by the heat from the horse. These must be replaced. Water – i.e. rain or saturation during cleaning – also causes leather to be hard and brittle. An overheated atmosphere or drying by direct heat have a similar affect.

Leatherwork should be rubbed clean, using a damp cloth or sponge which must be regularly rinsed out ● Only in the case of heavy mud – i.e. after a day's hunting – should it be necessary to use a wet cloth and more water. A chamois leather or dry cloth should then be used to dry off the leather ● Similarly, if leather has been exposed to heavy rain, it should first be cleaned, wiped with a cloth or chamois, and then allowed to dry out naturally. It should never be dried by placing near direct heat, or in a drying cupboard, as this destroys the natural oils.

● Using a slightly dampened sponge the saddle soap

should be well rubbed in, particularly on the fleshy or rough side of the leather where it is best absorbed • If leather has been very wet, a suitable leather dressing or neatsfoot oil should be applied to the flesh side when the leather is still damp and the pores are open. It will then be more thoroughly absorbed, will replace the oil and fat which has been lost, and will reduce the risk of any stiffening or cracking of the skin • When dry, it can be soaped • The outer surface of a saddle should not be greased or oiled, as it will stain the rider's breeches when it is next used • Similarly, unless a numnah is used, too much dressing or oil on the lining of a saddle can stain a horse's back, and a sensitive skin can become blistered • Leather which is stored often sweats, and becomes covered with mould spores. To prevent this, before putting away apply Vaseline or leather dressing and store in newspaper and/or a plastic bag. This will also prevent the drying out which can occur if leather is not in use • Care should be taken not to use excessive amounts of leather dressing or neatsfoot oil, as this can result in the leather becoming spongy and lacking in substance.

Equipment for Cleaning Saddlery:
- [ ] Saddle horse on which to rest the saddle.
- [ ] Bridle hook, preferably adjustable and with four hooks.
- [ ] Hooks for leathers and girths.
- [ ] Bucket, half full of tepid or cold water.
- [ ] Foam rubber sponge or rough cloth for washing.
- [ ] Foam rubber sponge for soaping.
- [ ] Sponge or small brush for applying neatsfoot oil or leather dressing. The latter can also be applied with the fingers.
- [ ] Bar of glycerine or tin of saddle soap.
- [ ] Tin of neatsfoot oil or other leather dressing.
- [ ] Metal polish and cloth, or Duraglit.
- [ ] Duster for polishing metalwork.
- [ ] Chamois leather. This is only necessary if the leather has been very wet. To use, wet the chamois then ring it out. Do not try to use it dry.

94

☐ Clean stable rubber or saddle cover to place over the saddle when finished.
☐ Horse hairs.
☐ Matchstick.

PROCEDURE FOR CLEANING SADDLES AND THEIR FITTINGS

The following notes apply to saddles with leather linings and Balding or Atherstone girths, leathers, irons and treads.

☐ Place the saddle on the saddle horse.
☐ Strip the saddle. Place the girth, leathers and stirrup irons including treads, on hooks. If the irons and treads are muddy, separate them and place them in the bucket of water.
☐ Upend the saddle and, using a damp wash cloth, rub the underneath of the saddle clean. Put a clean stable rubber on the saddle horse and place the saddle on it.
☐ After rinsing the cloth, clean the rest of the leather work, particularly any part which has been in contact with the horse's skin. Clean leather – usually the seat of the saddle – will not need washing.
☐ Wash the leathers and girth – especially the inside of any interleaving parts – the stirrup irons, and the treads.
☐ With brisk circular movements, using a very slightly dampened sponge, rub the soap liberally into all parts of the saddle flaps, the girth, and the leathers. Take care to move the buckle guards, so that the girth straps receive full attention. The top surface of the seat and saddle flap should then be wiped over with a dry cloth to avoid staining light breeches.
☐ Stainless steel irons can be rubbed over with a dry cloth and the treads replaced. They need regular but not daily cleaning with metal polish. Nickel irons, if they are to look bright, require polishing each day.

LINEN-LINED SADDLES. As above, but the lining should be washed after use in a similar way to leather. If the saddle is used for showing, a whitener is often put on round the edge of the lining.

SERGE-LINED SADDLES. As above, but if only slightly dirty, the lining when dry can be brushed clean with a dandy brush. A very dirty lining requires soaking and scrubbing. It may take a day or more to dry.

SIDE-SADDLES. Clean as above, but oil the stirrup device regularly.

Saddles which have been on clean horses with numnahs should be washed only infrequently; this way they will last longer • Girths and leathers however, should be carefully cleaned after use • Top surfaces of doeskin, suede or reversed cowhide, should never be treated with soap or leather dressing. They can be cleaned – i.e. the mud removed – by brushing with a soft clothes-brush or by wiping with a damp cloth. Should the surface wear smooth, it can be scuffed up with a wire shoe-brush or sandpaper; this, in time will reduce durability.

Girths

THREE-PLY LEATHER GIRTHS should be thoroughly cleaned, and then soaped or oiled. The inner felt lining must be regularly treated with neatsfoot oil, which will be absorbed into the flesh side of the leather, keeping it soft and supple.

NYLON, STRING, WEBBING or LAMPWICK GIRTHS. If they are dry, brush them clean. If muddy, and/or stained, soak them in warm detergent (making sure that any leather parts are not submerged), scrub them clean and thoroughly rinse them to remove detergent; if a horse is allergic to detergent, pure soap flakes should be used. Hang them up to dry by both buckle ends to prevent any rusting of the buckle tongues • Leather parts should be soaped or oiled • Girth buckles, and the metal studs and stirrup bars on saddles should be regularly cleaned with metal polish.

Pad Saddle and Felt Numnah
☐ Brush the felt with a dandy brush.
☐ When necessary, wash the underneath part with soap and a scrubbing-brush. Rinse thoroughly, and dry in a warm atmosphere.
☐ Keep free from hard knots of felt.
☐ Beware of moth damage and worn stitching.
☐ Clean leather and metal as already described.

Numnahs and Wither Pads
There are many different types. They must be kept clean, soft (no lumps), well aired, and in good repair ● Clean them according to makers' instructions, or as detailed for washing numnahs.

Washing Numnahs
SHEEPSKIN. Wash by hand in soap flakes. Thoroughly rinse and immediately apply warm glycerine or neatsfoot oil to the skin side. This prevents it becoming out of shape and hard.
SYNTHETIC SHEEPSKIN, QUILTED COTTON and LINEN-COVERED FOAM. Wash either by hand or by machine. Thorough rinsing is essential.
PLAIN FOAM RUBBER must be washed by hand.
● Leather fittings are likely to become dry and brittle. They should be well oiled and regularly tested. Numnahs with leather straps should not be machine washed.
● The skin of some horses will react to detergent, in which case, always use pure soap flakes and wash by hand.

Putting up a Saddle
For saddles in regular use:
☐ Put the irons on the leathers and put the stirrups back on the saddle. The irons should be run up the leathers, and then the leathers put through and under the irons.
☐ Place the girth flat on top of the saddle. With a three-ply girth the rounded edge should face towards the pommel.

☐ Place a cloth or cover on top of the saddle, and put the saddle up on its rack.

For saddles not in regular use, the girth leathers and irons should be hung separately on adjacent hooks, and the saddle should be put up without its fittings.

PROCEDURE FOR CLEANING BRIDLES

1. If Taking the Bridle to Pieces

☐ Hang the bridle on the cleaning hook.

☐ Remove the bits and curb chain. Put them in a bucket after removing the lip strap.

☐ Hang the reins over a hook.

☐ Take the bridle apart, memorising the buckle holes and the order in which the various headpieces are put together.

☐ Hang the leatherwork on a hook, or put it on a convenient work surface where it will not be likely to slip down to the floor.

☐ Thoroughly clean all leatherwork with a damp cloth.

☐ Wash and dry the bits and curb chain, and put them on a hook or on the work surface.

☐ Polish the bits, the curb chain, and then the bridle buckles and billet studs. The mouthpiece can be wiped over to remove any taste of metal polish. Finish with a dry, clean cloth.

☐ Soap all leatherwork, paying particular attention to folds and bends, which are all too easily missed in the daily cleaning.

☐ If the bridle has been wet, it may require an oil or leather dressing. Having treated the straps, fasten them at the bottom holes and runners. When the dressing has been absorbed, the bridle should be soaped and then put up correctly.

☐ When cleaning the headpiece, hold it firmly with one hand and use the cloth or sponge in the other hand.

☐ When cleaning the reins, step back from the bridle and

hold the reins taut. Wrap the cloth or sponge round each rein in turn, and clean them or apply soap by rubbing to and fro.

☐ When cleaning a bridle with stitched-on bits, do not put the bits in the water, to avoid wetting the sewn ends of the leatherwork. Where the leather is folded over the bit rings, insert neatsfoot oil or leather dressing to help preserve the leather and keep it supple.

Re-assemble the bridle in the following order:

1. Thread the short side of the headpiece through the off side of the browband and then the near side, making sure the throat lash is to the rear.
2. Place the headpiece on the hook.
3. For a double bridle, first thread the bridoon headpiece through the near side of the browband. It should go under the main headpiece and buckle on the off side.
4. First thread the noseband headpiece through the off side of the browband and buckle it on the near side. It should be on the under side of the headpiece.
5. Attach the two bit cheek pieces. On the double bridle, there should now be two buckles on each side of the headpiece.
6. Attach the bit and the bridoon to their respective headpieces. Make sure that the bit is not upside down. Attach the lip strap.
7. Place all straps in their keepers and runners.
8. Place the noseband round the bridle, and secure by a keeper and runner.
9. Replace the reins. On a double bridle they should be of different widths. The wider rein fixes on the bridoon. The narrower rein goes on the bit. The bridoon rein lies behind the bit rein.
10. The bridoon bit should lie a little above and over the front of the bit.
11. The lip strap on a double bridle should be pushed through the 'Ds' on the bit – from the inner side towards the outer side – and buckled on the near side. For neatness it should be threaded through the runner.

12. The curb chain can be hooked on, and should hang round the front of the bit with the lip strap ring hanging down.
13. Many people fasten the lip strap through the loose ring of the curb chain to avoid the latter being lost.

When putting a bridle together, buckle fastenings should be on the outside, and billeted fastenings on the inside of the headpiece and reins. The flesh side of the leather should be nearest to the horse's skin.

2. If Not Taking the Bridle to Pieces

☐ Hang the bridle on the cleaning hook. The buckle at the back of the noseband should be unfastened.
☐ Wash and dry the bit. A nickel bit will require polishing.
☐ Unfasten all buckles and put them in the bottom holes.
☐ Clean and soap all leatherwork, starting with the headpiece.
☐ Replace the buckles in the correct holes, with spare strap ends in their runners and keepers.
☐ Put the noseband round the outside of the bridle and thread it through the keepers.

A bridle which is used daily can be cleaned in the above manner. However, at least once a week it should be taken to pieces and given more thorough attention as already described.

AN ALTERNATIVE METHOD OF CLEANING TACK

You will require a foam-rubber sponge, saddle soap, a cloth and a bucket of warm water.

Method:
• Wet the sponge and rub the soap on it to establish a good lather.
• With the lathered sponge, wash all leather and metal work, making sure that all grease is removed from the leather. Add more water and soap to the sponge as necessary.

- Wipe dry.
- Blow away any foam remaining in the holes. If any is left, it will do no harm other than spoiling the appearance.
- For special occasions, competitions, etc. clean and soap as in the more elaborate procedure already described.

Putting Up a Bridle

If the bridle holder is high enough, it is better for the leather if the reins are allowed to hang down • The noseband should be put round the outside of the bridle and secured by the keeper and runner • The throat lash can be put round in a figure-of-eight, secured by a keeper and runner, but not buckled as this causes delay in using the bridle.

Alternative Methods

☐ Double up the reins at the back of the bridle. Put the throat lash through them, and then buckle or thread it through its keepers at the back.

☐ Double up the reins and wind the throat lash round them in a figure-of-eight. Put the throat lash round the front of the bridle and through the reins at the back. Then buckle or thread it through the keepers at the front.

General Notes

☐ Never balance the saddle on a narrow or unsteady surface – i.e. a pole or the back of a chair. The gullet may get damaged, and if the saddle falls, a broken or cracked tree and/or marked leather may result. If greater pressure is needed, place the saddle pommel down on top of your feet – never on the ground or on a hard surface – and work downwards.

☐ Use as little water as possible, but regularly rinse the wash cloth or sponge.

☐ Keep the soap sponge only slightly damp. If too wet, the soap will make lather and will lose its effectiveness, so that the leather remains dull.

☐ Never use hot water. Never use detergent or soda, unless for disinfectant purposes – e.g. for ringworm. All three may make cleaning easier, but they are very bad for the leather.

☐ Holes in stirrup leathers and bridles can become filled with soap and grease. Remove this with a matchstick or round nail.

☐ 'Jockeys', which are accumulations of black dirt and grease on the surface of the leather, can be removed by a fingernail or hairs from a horse's tail tied in a knot. Moisten the knotted horse hairs, cover in glycerine soap, and rub them over 'jockeys'. Never use a knife or any sharp instrument, as this will scratch and damage the surface of the leather.

☐ When undoing billet studs leave the end of the leather in the keeper and push it with the thumbs, so that the stud comes out of the leather. Then remove the leather from the keeper. When replacing it, put the end of the strap in the keepers and push the leather over the billet stud.

☐ If the buckles are stiff, it is easier to push the leather piece below the buckle upwards and through the buckle, rather than pulling the end of the strap up.

☐ During cleaning, inspect for wear all leatherwork, stitching and metalwork. The tongues of all buckles should be regularly greased; they are the most likely parts of the buckles to become worn and rusty.

CHECKING TACK FOR SOUNDNESS

The Saddle

The tree can be damaged or broken:
☐ If it is dropped on the ground.
☐ If it falls from a doorway or similarly unsafe position.
☐ If it slips off a horse's back before it is secured with a girth. If the girth is pulled to reach the girth straps, and the saddle is not held with the left hand, it can slip over the off side.
☐ If. it is left on the ground in the stable, and the horse steps on it.

☐ If a horse in the stable gets free, or is left free when saddled up, and rolls.
☐ If the horse falls and rolls over.
☐ If the rider catches hold of the cantle of a spring tree saddle when mounting.

A saddle with a narrow or medium tree can be strained by being used on a horse with a flat or wide wither.

Damage can occur in four places, the pommel or front arch, the waist, and at one or both points of the continuations of the front arch.

If damage to the tree is suspected or confirmed, the saddle should not be used but should be sent for immediate repair. A damaged tree can seriously injure a horse's back ● A fracture of the front arch or to the points can be mended ● Damage to the waist or cantle is more serious.

Other Areas Which Need Regular Checks
☐ The stitching of the girth straps.
☐ The stitching round the pocket.
☐ The holes in the girth straps.
☐ The girth straps.
☐ The saddle lining. If this is made of leather and is well looked after it should wear and stay smooth for many years. Linen lasts longer than serge, but both wear out in time. In all cases, the stitching requires checking as does the padding, which must be kept even so that there are no lumps which will give the horse a sore back.

The stitching on other parts of the saddle may give way, and look untidy, but the safety of the rider and the comfort of the horse should not be affected.

Parts of the Girth Which Need Regular Checks
☐ The suppleness and strength of the leather holding the buckles.
☐ The stitching of the leather round the buckles.

☐ The buckles and the wear of the buckle tongues. These must close firmly on the top part of the buckle. The buckles should be made of stainless steel.

☐ The strength of fabrics such as webbing, string and nylon, particularly in the buckle area.

☐ The front surface of a leather three-fold. This can crack and split, causing discomfort to the horse.

☐ The elastic inserts. These can become slack and unsafe.

Parts of the Leathers Which Need Checking

☐ The stitching round the buckle.

☐ The buckle itself, and the buckle tongues. Steel buckles are unlikely to break. Nickel is suspect and should not be used.

☐ The strength of the leather, and any stretching or signs of wear in the buckle holes. To avoid continual wear to the same areas, leathers can be shortened. This will bring the pressure on to a fresh piece of leather.

Stirrup Irons

Stainless steel irons are preferable. They are strong and sufficiently heavy, so rarely cause trouble – although if treads are not used, they will in time wear smooth on the base. All irons require careful checking for cracks.

Nickel irons are not recommended, as they: (1) crack and pull apart and (2) bend easily, lose shape and then break. When subjected to pressure, they can close and imprison the rider's foot – e.g. if a horse falls on its side, or if they are banged against a jump or gate.

THE BRIDLE

All stitching should be regularly examined and tested by stretching and pulling the leather.

Buckles and buckle tongues should be checked for wear. Buckles should be of stainless steel.

Reins should be checked for wear • Reins which have

been broken and then repaired should be closely examined. Unless the break was in the buckle area, the reins are only suitable for light work, as the stitching will be subjected to friction and strain ● Re-covered rubber reins are also suspect, as the re-stitching of the new rubber can weaken the rein ● Webbing, plaited cotton and linen-corded reins all wear more quickly than leather. They should not be patched, but must be replaced.

Bits

Particular points of wear are:
☐ The centre joints or joints of the mouthpiece.
☐ Where the rings or cheeks join the mouthpiece.

Nickel mouthpieces, rings and cheeks can become rough and/or sharp. Jointed snaffles can come apart at the joint.

Rubber and leather mouthpieces must be regularly checked for wear, as they have a limited life.

OTHER EQUIPMENT

Martingales, breastplates, and other leather or webbing equipment should all be checked for wear and tear. Particular attention should be paid to any buckle areas.

Lungeing tack. The centre ring of the cavesson receives constant pressure, and is subect to strain. It should be regularly checked. The lunge rein can deteriorate, and should be checked for weak places.

CHAPTER 8
Saddling Up and Unsaddling

SADDLING UP PROCEDURE

1. Collect the Bridle (which is assumed to be a snaffle)
Undo the throat lash and noseband ● If necessary, double up the reins to keep them clear of the ground ● Carry the bridle on the shoulder ● Collect the martingale (if used) and the boots.

2. Collect the Saddle
Check that it is complete, including buckle guards. If a numnah is to be worn, it should be put under the saddle and the straps fastened. Either:
☐ Place it on the lower arm with the pommel towards the elbow
or
☐ Place the cantle under the upper arm and hold the pommel with the same hand.
Take the required tack to the stable. On a wet day, cover the top of the saddle with a stable rubber. Place the saddle and bridle in a safe place.

3. Tie up the Horse
☐ Check that he is clean, his feet picked out, etc.
☐ Put on the boots.
It is usual to put the saddle on before the bridle.

106

4. Put on the Saddle

☐ Speak to the horse. Pat him on the neck and check that he is comfortably tied up, with the rope neither too tight nor too loose.

☐ Undo the rugs and then the roller or surcingles. Place the roller tidily in the corner or over the door. According to the temperature, either turn back the rugs or remove them. Fold them and put them with the roller.

☐ Put the saddle on the left arm • Approach the near side of the horse • Pat the saddle area and then, using both hands, place the saddle up on the withers, and slide it back to its correct position. Never move a saddle against the lay of the coat • Check the saddle numnah to ensure that the surface next to the horse's skin is smooth • Pull the numnah well up into the arch of the saddle • Attach the girth to the near side • Move round quietly under the horse's neck • Check the saddle on the off side and fasten the girth. This should be secure, but not tight. Make sure that skin is not wrinkled or caught up under the girth • Replace the rugs, but do not buckle them up, as if the rugs slip, it is better they fall clear than hang suspended round the horse's neck where they can frighten him and get torn • If restless horses are left, the rugs should be fastened and the roller replaced.

☐ If a martingale or breastplate is used, it should be put on before the saddle • Untie the horse • Put the neck strap over his head with the buckle on the near side • Re-tie the horse • Alternatively, unbuckle the martingale. Adjust it to the approximate length, and when doing up the girth, put it through the loop of the martingale • If two girths are used, fasten the one nearest the horse's elbow first. This is the one which should take the martingale • The second girth is placed on top and then buckled.

By putting the saddle on first, the horse's back has time to warm up before being ridden.

It is convenient and saves time if horses become accustomed to being saddled from the off side.

After girthing up before mounting, pull the horse's foot and leg forward to stretch the skin and ease any wrinkling.

When saddling up a young or nervous horse, it is advisable to untie the headcollar rope. But leave it through the loop. Should the horse resent or play up, there will be less chance of his pulling back and getting frightened. It is advisable that such an animal, once he is saddled, is not left unattended.

5. Put on the Bridle (For fitting see page 29.)
- ☐ Take the bridle and reins over the left arm, with the browband nearest to the elbow.
- ☐ Go up to the horse, talk to him, and stand behind his eye on the near side. Unfasten the headcollar and put it round his neck.
- ☐ Put the reins over the horse's head. At this stage, either of the two following methods can be used:
  1. Take hold of the headpiece of the bridle with the right hand ● Put the left hand under the bit and move the first finger around to the off side of the horse's mouth

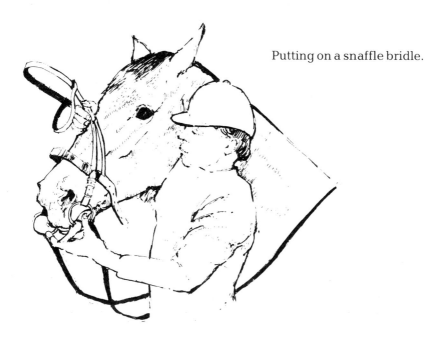

Putting on a snaffle bridle.

● Persuade him to open his mouth by inserting your first finger in the gap behind his front teeth ● As the horse opens his mouth, guide the bit into the mouth with your left hand and at the same time lift the bridle up towards the horse's ears with your right hand ● Once the bit is in his mouth, use your left hand to help the right hand move the bridle carefully over the horse's ears ● Ease out the mane and make it tidy, and put the forelock over the browband.

Check that the browband, noseband and bit are level. Adjust if necessary.

Fasten the throat lash and noseband. Put all the keepers into place and replace the headcollar.

2. This method can be used with horses who resist or raise their head when being bridled.
Hold the top of the bridle in the left hand ● Place the right hand under the horse's jaw and round to the front of his face ● Take hold of both cheek pieces of the bridle just below the browband ● Move the left hand to hold the bit ● Open the mouth with the left thumb, and continue the procedure as for 1.

To Put on a Double Bridle
● Undo the throat lash, noseband, curb chain and lip strap.
● Make sure the bridoon is on top and in front of the bit.
● Proceed as when putting on a snaffle bridle.
● When checking the bridle for fit, ensure that any alteration to the noseband or the bridoon does not make the bridle crooked. If this happens, hold the browband and pull the leather through it ● Fasten the curb chain and lip strap. See page 30, *Fitting a Double Bridle*.

Leaving a Saddled Horse
● If a saddled and bridled horse is to be left put the headcollar back over the top of the bridle. Double the reins twice round his neck, tie them in a knot on his withers or twist and loop them through the throat lash. If the reins are

put behind the stirrups they may upset a sensitive horse and cause an accident.

• A saddled horse should always be left tied up. If loose in the stable, he may get down and roll.

Carrying and Putting on a Side-Saddle

The saddle should be carried with the seat under the right arm, and with the right hand holding the top fixed pommel • Attach the girth and balance strap to the near side • Hold them with the flap strap – if there is one – and the stirrup iron in the left hand • Do not put them over a doeskin seat, or the stirrup iron over the top of the pommel, as this marks and wears the leather • The girth should be fastened high on the near side, and to the front two straps; any adjustments should be made on the off side • Fasten the balance strap to the angled strap. Do not buckle it too high, as it lies under the right calf of the rider.

• Place the saddle on the horse's back from the near side, as for a normal saddle • Fasten the girth on the off side. The balance strap must lie over the top of the girth, and should then be brought across and fastened on the near off side. It must not be too tight. Then fasten the flap strap, which comes on top. It must never be tighter than the girth and balance strap • When moving round the horse, try to ensure the saddle is held firm by a second person.

• If a martingale is used, all three straps should go through it.

• When checking a saddle for fit, make sure that it sits evenly on the horse's back and does not sit too far up on the withers • The points of the tree must stay clear of the shoulder, or the saddle will rock about. • For a saddle to sit well, the horse must have a good wither. Note that a horse's back requires some time to become hardened to the unaccustomed weight and shape of the side-saddle.

• Before mounting, the rider should check the girth. The balance strap should not be too tight nor too far back, as this may cause the horse to buck.

• When the rider is mounted, the girth and balance strap should be adjusted from the off side.

Care of the Side-Saddle

☐ If possible, bring the horse out of the stable before saddling. If he is saddled in the stable, ensure that the lower pommel does not catch on the door as the horse is led out, and also when he is led back in.

☐ Once the saddle is on and girthed up, avoid turning the horse sharply, as this can crack the tree.

☐ The saddle must never be left on the horse with the girths unfastened, unless he is held by another person.

☐ Never transport the horse in a horse box or trailer wearing a side-saddle.

☐ When unsaddling, do not put the girth and back strap across the seat as the doeskin is easily marked.

☐ Never rest a saddle on a door or insecure surface.

☐ If it has to be put on the ground, place it down pommel first.

UNSADDLING

There are several accepted methods of unsaddling. The following is the normal procedure:

1. On dismounting, run up the irons on the leathers and ease the girth one or two holes.
2. Take the reins over the horse's head, lead him into his stable, and close the door.
3. Take up the headcollar and place it round the horse's neck with the rope untied.
4. Unfasten the throat lash, the noseband and – if there is one – the curb chain. If there is a standing martingale, release it. If there is a running martingale, unfasten the reins, and release it.
5. With your right hand, ease the bridle over the horse's head, at the same time steadying his face and then

111

taking the bridle with your left hand. The horse must be allowed time to quietly let go of the bit.

6. Place the bridle over your left arm so that both hands are free to put on the headcollar and to tie up the horse.
7. Place the bridle over your shoulder.
8. Unfasten the girth. If there is a martingale, take it out of the loop. Lift the saddle, draw it over the horse's shoulder and place it on your left arm. The girth can be put over the top of the saddle, but if the girth is wet or muddy, leave it down. The martingale neck strap should be undone, and the martingale should be placed, with the bridle, on your shoulder.
9. Put the saddle and bridle on, or outside, the stable door. If you put the saddle on the ground, place the pommel down first, with the girth between the wall and the cantle; this prevents the leather from being marked or scratched. If you put the saddle on the door, make sure that it will not be knocked off.
10. Return to the horse, and briskly pat the saddle area to restore circulation.
11. Replace the rugs.
12. If the horse is wet, or is unlikely to break out, put either a sweat rug or straw underneath the rugs.
13. Take the saddle and bridle to the tack room ready for cleaning. Mud will come off easily if it is sponged when still wet.

An alternative procedure is to take the saddle off first, as detailed in 8, 9 and 10 above. Then remove the bridle as in 3, 4, 5 and 6 above. This method can be useful for restless horses, who are better controlled in a bridle.

Procedure after Unsaddling
1. Pick out the feet.
2. If the feet are muddy, wash them. Take care not to wet the heels.
3. Check the legs.
4. Sponge off any sweat marks. On a hot day, the horse can be washed off out of doors.

5. Check for any signs of rubbing in the saddle, girth and mouth areas.
6. If the horse is wet put on a sweat sheet *and* walk him dry.
7. Tie up the haynet.
8. Groom horse – or at least brush off sweat marks.
9. Replace all the rugs.
10. Refill the water bucket.

Bibliography

BRITISH HORSE SOCIETY, *Manual of Horsemanship* (Threshold Books).

HARTLEY EDWARDS, ELWYN, *Saddlery* (J.A. Allen).

MACDONALD, JANET, AND FRANCIS, MRS V., *Riding Side Saddle* (Pelham Books).

TUKE, DIANA, *Bit by Bit* (J.A. Allen).

TUKE, DIANA, *Stitch by Stitch* (J.A. Allen).

Horse and Hound Survey.

Index

Index

NOTES

NOTES

NOTES

NOTES

NOTES

NOTES

NOTES

NOTES